BELOVED

* * *

"Donald Schmidt has written a moving memoir of a gay Christian traversing the political and cultural landscape of the late 20th and early 21st centuries. Along the way, he encounters both homophobia and moments of profound acceptance. As a gay man, he gives personal dimension to a central theme of his work — that sexual orientation is much more about identity and relationship than it is about outward appearances and individual acts. This is particularly true when he describes being in the midst of the AIDS crisis in the 1980s. Throughout the narrative, the personal stories of love and loss are undergirded by Schmidt's sense of self-deprecating humour and profound biblical witness. This latter gift is particularly manifest when he counters homophobic use of questionable proof texts with the profound story of Philip and the Ethiopian eunuch in the book of Acts. In the end, one is left with a story that is both brutally honest and immensely grace filled."

– Rev. Brian Thorpe, United Church of Canada, British Columbia

"I want to shout to the world: read this book! Schmidt's powerful writing brought back memories of my own life that I had forgotten. Reading it made me laugh, and cry, and think, and reflect. Reading this book is like eating a delicious meal — you have to finish it all without stopping. For anyone who is gay or thinks they may be this is a must-read. And for those in their family who do not share the same orientation I think it is a must-read as well."

– Rev. Fred Gilbert, United Methodist Church, Florida

BELOVED

Being Gay and Christian

DONALD SCHMIDT

* * *

WOOD LAKE

Editor: Mike Schwartzentruber
Proofreader: Dianne Greenslade
Designer: Robert MacDonald
Author photograph: Val Carson

Library and Archives Canada Cataloguing in Publication
Title: Beloved : being gay and Christian / Donald Schmidt.
Names: Schmidt, Donald, 1959- author.
Identifiers: Canadiana (print) 20220398984 | Canadiana (ebook) 20220399042 | ISBN 9781773436388 (softcover) | ISBN 9781773436395 (HTML)
Subjects: LCSH: Schmidt, Donald, 1959- | LCSH: Christian gays – Canada – Biography. | LCSH: Gay clergy – Canada – Biography. | LCSH: United Church of Canada – Clergy – Biography. | LCSH: AIDS (Disease) – Social aspects – Québec (Province) – Montréal – History – 20th century. | LCSH: Gay community – Québec (Province) – Montréal – History – 20th century. | LCSH: Christian biography – Canada. | LCGFT: Autobiographies.
Classification: LCC BX9883.S36 A3 2022 | DDC 287.9/2092 – dc23

Copyright © 2022 Donald Schmidt
All rights reserved. No part of this publication may be reproduced – except in the case of brief quotations embodied in critical articles and reviews – stored in an electronic retrieval system, or transmitted in any form or by any means, electronic, mechanical, photocopying, recording, or otherwise, without prior written permission of the publisher or copyright holder.

ISBN 978-1-77343-638-8

Published by Wood Lake Publishing Inc.
485 Beaver Lake Road, Kelowna, BC, Canada, V4V 1S5
www.woodlake.com | 250.766.2778

Wood Lake Publishing acknowledges the financial support of the Government of Canada.
Wood Lake Publishing acknowledges the financial support of the Province of British Columbia through the Book Publishing Tax Credit.

Wood Lake Publishing acknowledges that we operate in the unceded territory of the Syilx/Okanagan People, and we work to support reconciliation and challenge the legacies of colonialism.
The Syilx/Okanagan territory is a diverse and beautiful landscape of deserts and lakes, alpine forests and endangered grasslands. We honour the ancestral stewardship of the Syilx/Okanagan People.

GOLD

Printed in Canada
Printing 10 9 8 7 6 5 4 3 2 1

If you have been told that God is some
kind of punishing, capricious, angry
bastard with a killer surveillance system
who is basically always disappointed
with you for being a human being
then you have been lied to.
The church has failed you.
— NADIA BOLZ-WEBER

* * *

My morality and faith are choices.
My sexual orientation however isn't.
— ANTHONY VENN-BROWN

* * *

God is love,
And love *is* a relationship.
This relationship is one of joy,
and it can't be contained.
— ROB BELL

PREFACE

In this book I set out to share some stories about what it was like growing up when I did – the 1960s to the 1980s – as a gay man who is also Christian, or as a Christian who happens to be gay. The stories do not form a single, linear narrative but are snippets from memories and lost hopes that now, safely on this side of survival, one can dare to recall. All the names (except that of my husband, Kevin) have been changed because people have the right to tell their own stories in their own way. But the stories are all real. They are about things that happened or about things that could have been had circumstances been different. They speak about destroyed realities. They come from life.

I dedicate this book to the many others – often silenced by death, or by the church, or by society – who have made similar journeys, or who at least have attempted them. It's not always been an easy transit, and if I wore a hat I would gladly take it off to honour them.

I offer my sincere thanks to Alyson, Fred, and Paul who helped jog my memory on some of the events that shaped my narrative, and who filled in pieces that were beginning to fade. I also thank the wonderful community of folks at Wood Lake Publishing – Patty, Debbie, Mike, and Robert – for their commitment to telling the real faith story of the Christian church.

INTRODUCTION

I knew I was different. And I knew I was a Christian. Over time, those two aspects of my identity merged, sometimes. At other times, they clashed. But they were always present, dancing in some strange kind of way across the years and then decades of my life.

I had people tell me I had no right to be gay if I was a Christian, or conversely to call myself a Christian if I was gay. I have had people try to "convert" me or "heal" me, and people who have been downright hostile toward me. Some have even tried to deny my calling as a minister and prevent me from collecting my pension.

I have fought for my rights and for the rights of others and have been kicked to the proverbial curb many times for my efforts. Yet through it all, two constants remain:

I am gay. That is a reality that has been true since before I was born and is never going to change – no matter what someone else might want, or how fervently they might want it.

I have a passionate love affair with my Creator, and with Jesus Christ, and believe that God loves me and calls me to work for justice and goodness in the world. Again, this will not change for me – although at times that love affair gets a little deeper and stronger, at other times seems a bit more distant.

This book is about my discovery and eventual acceptance of who I am – which was not easy, considering I grew up in an era when being gay was not something one could talk about or celebrate.

Over time the situation has changed and I am extremely grateful that for many people today it is safe to be open about their sexuality, but in my younger years there was only one option, and that one option was heterosexuality. If that was not who you were, well, you just made things work however you could. And you never talked about it. Ever.

I cannot tell my story without confronting the reality of AIDS, which dominated the gay community for much of the 1980s and is still a very real and threatening thing in our world. It didn't help that some people thought AIDS was a divine punishment on the LGBTQ+ community for being who we were. That twisted idea got more complicated and difficult to hold when increasing numbers of people who were *not* gay caught AIDS and died from it. Of course, reality seldom shuts up fanaticism for very long, but it helps the rest of us keep things in perspective.

I have organized this book in – roughly – chronological order. That said, I do jump around a bit, because that's how memory works. And sometimes events are related to each other even though they occurred at points wildly disconnected by time. The book is subjective, originating solely from what I can recall. But in that there is, I hope and trust, a certain degree of raw honesty.

BELOVED

I was born in 1959. In more recent years, my mother has frequently mentioned that the first time she held me she knew I was different. For many years she didn't know *how* I was different, she just knew that I was. As time went on, however, she came to understand that her intuitive sense was related to my sexuality. How she knew that when I was an infant in her arms is quite beyond me. Yet I also somehow *do* get it. I have sometimes looked at someone and had thoughts, fleeting perhaps but still significant, that there was *something* about them.

* * *

The 1960s were fun and crazy years to grow up in – something many people know better than I, since I was still a young child. Things were changing at a rapid pace, everywhere you turned. Values and truths and stories from the not-so-distant past were being flung aside by those who wanted new values, new truths, and new stories.

There were wars (in Vietnam certainly, but also in Biafra and at times in the Middle East) that told me of a world in huge conflict. There was a sexual revolution that I was aware of, even long before I really had anything more than the vaguest idea what sex even was. And people were being shot – John F. Kennedy, Martin Luther King Jr, and Robert Kennedy. Each of those assassinations seemed to put an end to whatever had gone before, and left people grasping at what the next moment might hold.

For Canadians, the decade essentially ended with the October Crisis in 1970, when members of the Front de Liberation du Quebec kidnapped two dignitaries: British trade commissioner James Cross and Quebec cabinet minister Pierre Laporte. They killed Laporte, and I often think that in that moment Canada had to scramble to redefine itself. After a smug decade when we could point to riots and assassinations in the United States and think ourselves better, suddenly we had to confront the reality that we were not immune. It was a painful and humbling experience for many.

Not much of this touched me directly, of course, but it certainly helped shape me and define me, and in the process told me a lot about the world.

* * *

I date a lot of things in my life around the pivotal event of my family's move, in 1964, from Victoria, British Columbia (a modest and, at that point, rather backward little city on Vancouver Island) to Crofton, about 80 km (50 mi) north. I categorize things as happening either before we moved or after we moved.

Using that guidepost, I know I was aware of a simple truth early on; before I turned five I already knew I found men beautiful. Really beautiful. I also already sort of knew that I was supposed to find women beautiful. Occasionally, people would make a comment or suggestion about a woman's beauty (never about a man's) and I picked up early that, someday, I would fall in love with a beautiful woman and marry her and live happily ever after. But I also knew that men were beautiful. I would see men and fantasize about holding them, about cuddling them. I knew nothing about sex but that didn't matter. I loved men.

I say this because some people think sexual orientation — that is, whether we are gay or straight — is about sex. It's not.

Sex is part of it, because sex is part of a healthy adult life, but being homosexual or heterosexual is 99 per cent of the time *not* about sex – it's about identity. I am gay, but sex is a very small part of my life considering there are 24 hours in a day. Being gay is about how I see the world, how I live in the world, and how I want to relate to the world – not just in sexual terms, but in regards to *everything*.

This can be a little difficult for people who are straight to understand, because we live in a very straight-dominant society. Most of our advertising, most of our imaging, most of our conversation, most of our stories – these all centre around a heterosexual approach to life. Fortunately, this is changing. Increasingly, advertising includes gay and lesbian couples. The approach is nonchalant, casual, and has nothing to do with sex. Couples are merely shown relating to one another, interacting with one another. Of course homosexual characters and relationships are much more prominent now in television and movies also, even if they are not the "norm."

The key point I want to make is that I knew very early on that I found men beautiful and, to the extent that I imagined my future, I saw myself in a relationship with a man because, well, that's what seemed normal and natural to me.

My imaginings would not really have mattered except that at some point I must have said something, however innocently, about finding a certain man attractive, at which point I was told in kind but extremely firm words that little boys were not supposed to think like that. I tried not to, but it was hard.

* * *

When we lived in Victoria, we went to church and Sunday school. My father had grown up Baptist and my mother was nominally Anglican, so they compromised and attended the United Church (a blend of Congregationalists, Presbyterians, and Methodists formed in 1925). I remember dressing up in a jacket and tie and going to St. Aidan's United Church. I remember, too, being baptized there, which happened when I was three and a half. My baptism probably qualifies as my earliest actual memory, which might help explain my later career choice.

I was baptized in November along with my sister. We were given small copies of the New Testament and a flower, which I would say was a daffodil, except it was November.

I clearly remember coming away from my baptism – or christening as it tended to be called in those days – with a profound sense that I belonged to God, and that God loved me, and that no one could ever take that away from me. That was all pretty cool – even though I had no real understanding of who or what "God" was – perhaps some kind of invisible being that lived up in the sky somewhere and had something to do with Christmas, although not with the presents because they came from Santa Claus, but who *definitely* had something to do with Easter. Granted, I didn't understand Easter either. As I grew older, though, it took on greater and greater significance for me. *God must really love us to bring Jesus back from the dead for us*, I thought.

* * *

I remember going to a bazaar at my sister's school before we moved to Crofton. She was two years older than me and had started Grade 1 when I was four. I was at this event with my parents, and at one point I was with my father at the "fishpond." That was the activity where you paid five cents and cast a fishing line over a short wall. Someone on the other side would ask if you were a boy or a girl and then tie a cheap novelty item to the end of the line, which you drew up to see what kind of treasure you had snagged.

Something must have happened in the communication, because what I got was a miniature plastic tea set, the kind one would use when playing dolls. I was thrilled! However, when one of the organizers noticed that a boy had gotten this entirely inappropriate toy she apologized, took the tea set away from me, and gave me a rubber ball instead. I was clearly supposed to have been greatly relieved and full of appreciation, but I proceeded to bawl at what I have been told was a horrendous volume. I wanted the tea set. I didn't know any differently — that boys were *not* supposed to want doll things, girl's things, feminine things. I just knew how thrilled I had been when I got it, and how devastated I was when they took it away from me.

The astonishing thing in all this was my father, an otherwise prototypical, meat-and-potatoes eating, mill-working male. It would be reasonable to expect that he wanted nothing more than for his male child to reject the tea set and be thrilled with the rubber ball. But when I protested, he came to my defence. I clearly remember — as if it had happened just last week — my father saying to the woman at the fishpond that if I wanted the tea set, which after all they had given me, they should let me have it.

As we walked away, I held my dad's hand with one of mine, and clutched the plastic tea set with the other. I remember thinking how proud I was that this was my dad, and that he had stood up for me. I knew I would be safe as long as he was looking out for me. Over the years this feeling ebbed and flowed, but over all it has won out.

* * *

Years later, my father's brother, who was a Baptist minister, heard that I was gay. In what I assume he meant in a kindly way, he offered to "fix" me. He claimed that after a week with him I would be "good as new" (an odd turn of phrase in this context). To their credit, both of my parents rejected his offer outright. My father even got hostile with him, telling him he could keep his arrogant ideas to himself. I didn't need "fixing" and frankly it was a dumb idea.

I can only commend my father for this, because I know that he never planned, hoped, or dreamed of having a gay son. Yet when that's what the universe dealt him, he found ways to accept me. No, I would never go moose hunting with him and would never quite enjoy hockey to the extent he did. But over time he came to respect that I was his son, that I was not going away, and that I was not going to change.

Similarly, my mother had a friend with whom she corresponded regularly. At some point my mother happened to mention that I was gay. This friend hit the roof and felt compelled to write my mother a lengthy letter in which she quoted numerous biblical texts (always wildly out of context) that showed I was going to go to hell unless I changed. My mother responded by saying that if this was the best her friend could come up with, then she could keep her nasty ideas to herself. If this meant they could no longer be friends, then so be it.

As far as I know, they still exchange Christmas cards.

* * *

I admire my parents immensely when I think of these two incidents. They are of a generation for whom having a gay son could not have been easy. On the other hand, they were always proud to defend the rights of the proverbial underdog and, in this instance, they felt I fit that category well. I had a right to exist and to be who I was, and neither they nor anyone else had a right to interfere. They also came to believe that the God whom they worshipped would never make people that were destined for hell.

Their belief in turn helped shape my own theology, and I will be eternally grateful.

* * *

While I found men beautiful, I also found them very intimidating. I felt strangely uncomfortable around my dad's friends when they would come over, I think because I knew I didn't fit in. I knew I was different, and I knew that this difference had to do with men, but I could not put my finger on what it was, exactly, even though it was there, and it was real.

After we moved and as I grew older, my dad and I would sometimes go fishing with other men and their sons. We even went on a few camping trips – just the "guys." I always felt a little uncomfortable. Men fascinated me and terrified me. They made me feel comfortable and uncomfortable at the same time.

* * *

I have a horrible memory fragment from the spring of the year I turned seven. Something happened at the birthday party of a friend of mine. I cannot recall the details (which is why I call it a memory fragment) but enough of the other pieces give me a sense of what probably happened.

In those days in a small town, you walked everywhere, so I had walked to Tommy's party – he only lived about a quarter mile down the street anyway. I walked to the party, but I ran home afterwards.

My mother says I came in the door crying and ran to my room. When she asked what was wrong, I screamed something like "I don't want to talk about it – ever!" and flew into a rage of angry tears face down on my bed.

A few days later my parents had to take me to the doctor

because I was severely constipated — there were some pretty serious tears in my anus and it was so painful I couldn't go to the bathroom.

It was 1966. It was a small town.

I am quite sure that nowadays the reaction of parents and doctors would be to assume that a sexual assault had taken place. Today, an investigation would likely be launched, and gentle questions would be asked to draw out what might have transpired at the party. But in 1966 in a small town there was none of that.

I distinctly remember (some 55 years later) the doctor and my parents agreeing that it was a mystery as to how this could have happened, and the doctor suggesting a variety of medical things to take care of the anal tears in short order. The wounds actually took months to heal, but I remember lying about it and hiding the fact as best I could. No one seemed to object to the fact that we could pretend nothing was really wrong, or that nothing had happened.

Tommy and his family moved away about a month later. Apparently, his dad got a job rather suddenly somewhere else. I knew I would miss my friend. But I also remember feeling a relief I could never put my finger on.

Other than fragments, I have no real memory of what happened at that party. But it seems clear that my friend's father did something brutally inappropriate to me and I'm willing to bet I was hardly his first victim. I probably was not the last, either. Not unless the man was later arrested.

Or shot.

* * *

I have always hesitated to tell that story. Not because it's shameful — I mean, some might see it that way, but I don't. I did nothing wrong. I was just shy of seven years old. What could I have done?

No, the reason I have always hesitated is because I don't want people to jump to the conclusion that this incident had anything to do with my sexual orientation. "Gee, no wonder he's queer — couldn't help it if someone raped him when he was just a wee lad."

It just isn't true.

I know — as much as I know how to breathe — that I was gay from the day I was born. No one taught me, no one converted me, no one took me to that place through a sick act of child molestation. I was always gay.

I remember when I was very little — probably around four years old — seeing a man, a beautiful man, and wishing I could hold him and just be held by him and be with him forever, because he was so beautiful. Lots of men have told me similar stories — except theirs generally involved beautiful women.

* * *

As I grew older, I fell in love with hockey players (it was small town Canada — watching hockey games with your father was almost required by law) and with other beautiful men I saw in passing. I looked for men modelling bathing suits and underwear in the Eaton's catalogue and wished I could somehow wave a wand and remove the snippets of clothing they were wearing.

In the beginning, I thought it was okay. I mean, how does a child know that something that feels perfectly natural — that they didn't decide on, but just happened — is not exactly what everyone else seemingly feels, or what you're "supposed" to feel.

It was only later, when I learned the meaning behind that dreaded word "homo," that I knew I didn't really want to be one of *those* people, because they got beaten up, and people looked down their noses at them, and worse.

* * *

Growing up, I knew I was different. I also knew there was no one I could talk to. That's one of the hardest parts of growing up gay. Some kids are lucky, of course, and they have parents who are also gay, or an aunt or uncle who is gay, or at least *someone* with a very understanding and empathetic ear. At the other end of the spectrum, though, are the countless ones who fear that if they tell their parents anything honest about their sexual identity, they'll pay a huge price for it. Of course, while a few of these people are pleasantly surprised and receive some measure of acceptance and support, the majority have their fears confirmed when they are kicked out of the house, told they are going to hell, made to feel guilty simply for being honest about who they are, and sometimes even worse.

I didn't think I would be cast out – my parents had clearly established a threshold of unconditional love, and I was pretty sure I could never sink below it – but still I found it hard to talk to them about it. What I wanted was a gay best friend who I could talk to and share those "dark" secrets we share as we begin to discover ourselves. I envy so much all those people – gay, straight, and in-between – who have a soulmate when they're growing up. I mean, I did okay without one, and I had some very close friends, many of whom are still my friends today. But it would have been wonderful to have someone I could discuss my feelings of difference with.

* * *

I remember once – only once, mind you – walking with my boyfriend Geoff in New York City. This would have been in the 1980s. I can't remember which part of the city he wanted to show me, but we were walking down some non-famous part of a non-famous street, and we held hands.

I probably would not have done it, but Geoff had said that one of the many things he loved about New York was that you could walk down the streets holding hands and no one would care. So we did.

It felt a little strange, and I spent the first few minutes wondering if anyone would beat us up. When no one did, I relaxed, and as we continued to walk I thought how wonderful it was to do such a simple thing. It felt good. It felt right.

But that was the '80s, like I said. In the 1960s and early 1970s, it seemed very far from possible.

* * *

In the 1970s there was a lot of ambiguity about a lot of things. The world was still trying to figure out how to move on from the 1960s – how much change to embrace, and how much to try to roll back.

For the gay community, the signature event that closed off the 1960s was Stonewall. It is sometimes called the Stonewall Riot or Stonewall Uprising, and it took place at the end of June in 1969. You can find far more details on the Internet than I'll offer here, but basically it was the night the gay community in New York City told the police, "We've had enough!"

If you've ever spent the summer in an eastern North American city (take your pick of New York, Montreal, Boston, Toronto, etc.) you will know that they can get very hot and muggy in the evening, and that this has an effect on people. Some turn angry, some get fatigued more easily, some are just plain restless. All of these, I'm sure, contributed to what happened at the Stonewall Inn.

Four police officers attempted a raid on the Stonewall, a well-known gay bar in New York. There were literally about

500 LGBTQ+ folks in the bar and surrounding area, and so it really was not the brightest tactical move on the part of the police. Except that in the past, folks in the LGBTQ+ community tended to cower in fear and skulk away quietly whenever the authorities turned up. Not this time.

As the police announced their raid and the lights came on in the bar, people stood their ground. They pushed the police aside and went outside. The officers called for reinforcements and soon there was a large and angry group of LGBTQ+ folks outside, and some police barricaded inside. The mob outside kept yelling to the police "Come out! Come out!" – an irony that has not been lost on many.

While that first riot was controlled by 4 a.m., the next night a much larger number of folks from the LGBTQ+ community showed up, and over time the broader community realized that it was no longer going to be as easy as it had been to push LGBTQ+ folks aside. They were tougher than anyone had thought at first, and they were not going to take any more abuse. For many in the LGBTQ+ community this was the night everything changed, and it is why most Pride marches and celebrations take place in June, to commemorate this watershed moment.

I didn't know anything about Stonewall at the time – I was only 11 – but I began to hear the word "gay" bandied about in various conversations in ways that made me wonder. I didn't know exactly what it was I was wondering about, but the word held some kind of intrigue. I knew that it meant more than it once had, that it no longer referred to being happy. It had something to do with being homosexual and, as I moved into adolescence, I knew that somehow it had something to do with me.

**

Early in the 1970s, in my early teens, I experienced a call to ministry. Our local United Church offered a more contemporary worship service at 9 a.m. and even invited laypersons to lead the worship. I leapt at the chance! It felt so wonderful to be able to develop a theme, add songs to it, and make it work as a service. I dare to think now how primitive my efforts undoubtedly were, but they were a powerful experience for me. Looking at scripture, exploring it, and finding ways to make it come alive for others – this felt so good. I knew this was what I wanted to do. And I knew it was what God wanted me to do, even if I was only about 13.

At the time – and this is a good thing – I was far too naïve to think that anything about my identity would prevent me from entering the ministry. I mean, why wouldn't the church want me? God did.

* * *

I got beaten up a lot in high school because I found I couldn't lie about myself.

I'm not sure I really knew I was gay, but I liked to wear a brightly coloured scarf around my throat, and I intentionally took on some feminine mannerisms. That was not an acceptable thing for a boy to do in the 1970s – not where I lived – and so I got beaten up. Nothing horrible or bloody, but I don't think a day went by when somebody didn't shove me up against the lockers, push my books out of my arm, or kick me when I was on my hands and knees picking them up.

It came to a head when my guidance counsellor – who was a real bastard – threatened to suspend me. "You're a nuisance," he began. "It's the, the way you carry yourself. If you can't change – if you won't change – then we'll have no choice. You're provoking the other students."

I was provoking *them?* *They* were beating *me* up!

One of the boys who did it the most was the counsellor's own son. Surely the counsellor knew that! Was this really about defending his son against some "faggot," I wondered.

This was one of many times when the world told me my place, and the consequences of living in that place. Become normal or pay the price. It was simple. Except that for someone like me, it wasn't simple.

* * *

I am left-handed. As far as anyone can tell me, I was born that way. But it didn't stop the school from trying to change me. When we learned cursive writing, the book that was used showed how to form the letters with poise, style, and great flourish. Except if you were left-handed you couldn't do it. It was impossible, unless you turned your arm around so that your hand was in this godawful position that was, basically, upside down, so you could replicate holding the pen in your right hand.

I know kids who did that; one of them was still writing that way well into adulthood.

But I couldn't. I couldn't conform to such nonsense. Why? Because I could form quite suitable and quite legible letters without compromising my hand. Perhaps I was not the only rebel in this regard, because when I hit Grade 4 they stopped using that textbook. I never looked back – I wrote the way I wanted.

Years later, someone did grapho-analysis on my handwriting. She had not known me as a child, but looked at my sample and said, "You taught yourself to write. I'm guessing when you were quite young."

My handwriting secret was out.

That whole experience told me that if I was going to survive in this life, I had to not just write the only way I could but *live* the only way I could. If it meant being beaten up, so be it. If it meant being laughed at, so be it. The world would have to get used to me.

Thankfully, it became a lot easier when, after high school, I moved 4,000 kilometres away.

* * *

One thing I've never been able to understand is the fear many straight men seem to have that gay men are going to put the make on them, or worse. So let me be clear – and I say this on behalf of 99.99 percent of gay men worldwide: I am gay. I am queer. I am a shirt lifter, and a friend of Dorothy. I play for the other team, I bat for the other side, and I walk down the other side of the street. In short, I am a homosexual.

But I am not a rapist.

I have no desire to sleep with you if you have no desire to sleep with me – it really is that simple.

Many straight men (married or single) may see a woman and make some comment like, "I wouldn't mind hopping into the sack with her." Frankly, a lot of men might say something much cruder than that. But I don't imagine that the vast majority of these men have any intention of taking it further. To be sure, it's a thoughtless, sexist, and potentially violating comment. The issue here, of course, is not whether it's *appropriate* or not; my point is that these are *words*, not *actions*.

The same is true for the many gay men who will make a comment about another man. Trust me, we aren't interested if you're not interested. We're not out to "convert" you because, as we have been saying for centuries, we know that one's sexuality cannot change.

But none of that means you're not attractive.

***

There were pieces of music that made me feel uncomfortable. One of them was the Beatles' "Get Back." It was a song I particularly liked, but I was always nervous listening to it with (straight) adults around. The line "Sweet Loretta Martin thought she was a woman, but she was another man" struck a little too close to home. If I sang along or even just tapped my foot to the beat, would people think I harboured some sense of sexual ambiguity?

Worse still was the song "Lola" by the Kinks. It was about someone who was transgender or at least a transvestite who "walked like a woman but talked like a man." I loved the song, and I felt an attraction not just to the tune but also secretly to the words. Again, I was too young to fully understand them, but there was something inviting and mysterious about gender fluidity, and about people being non-binary — words that meant nothing then, although the concepts were real.

***

I didn't particularly enjoy my teens, and I wanted to get them done and over with as soon as possible. I was going to learn to drive, get a car, and go somewhere. Where? It didn't matter. Just somewhere. I was going to get away — and in so doing I could leave behind any judgmental eyes that might question my tastes in music, clothing, or who I wanted to go to bed with.

Given the era and the fact that I lived on an island that tended to lag, socially at least, several years behind the rest of the world, and because of the fear of actually *saying* what (or who) you wanted, I assumed that I would find a nice girl, and we'd fall in love and get married and have babies. It's what you did.

Except I didn't really want a girl. I fantasized about boys. I saw guys who were drop-dead gorgeous and as my sexuality blossomed so did my interest in imagining things I might do with them. It was only natural — adolescent boys have sexual fantasies every 2.4 seconds, apparently — except that my interest was in people of my own gender, and somewhere not-so-deep inside I knew I was supposed to think it was wrong. I wasn't quite sure *why* it was supposed to be wrong, but I knew that's what most people thought. There were certainly enough things in the overall culture to tell me that.

Sometimes, these attitudes were spoken, such as when someone referred to anyone who was vaguely effeminate as a "homo," which was pretty bad; or as a "faggot" or "fag," which was substantially worse. "Queer" also got used and generally was as bad as faggot except it had the added problem of still being used in mainstream vocabulary to mean "odd" without anything sexual attached to it. I remember one of my friends whose mother always referred to me as "That queer Donald Schmidt," and we never knew for sure on what level she meant it.

But it didn't matter. You knew that being called any of those words — homo, faggot, queer — was not a good thing, and if you got called them too often the names would stick, and you could probably never scrape them off again. (See appendix for more explanation of some of the terms used to describe different sexual and gender identities over the years.)

* * *

There were a couple other boys in high school who regularly got called "faggot." One of them was very effeminate, and the other one was perhaps also effeminate, but not to the same degree. He probably could have gotten away with being seen as straight except that he liked Elton John and, while the singer wouldn't come out for years, he was generally thought of as gay even in the early '70s.

How I wanted to talk to those guys. How I wished we could have formed a little society that could talk about the things we needed to talk about. But I knew we couldn't, and I think they knew it, too. It would have been way, way too risky. Even to be seen talking to them put you in a dangerous position. So I ignored them and they ignored me. To this day I wonder what became of them, and whether they knew I was "like them" or not.

And I wonder if they were as lonely as I was.

***

I did have a boyfriend in high school. Mercifully, Charles was a few years older than me so after one year of Junior High when we overlapped in the same school, we were never at the same place at the same time. I say "mercifully" because had we hung out together who knows what might have happened and whether we would have survived or not. On rural Vancouver Island, boys with boys was a definite no-no in the 1970s. Maybe it was okay elsewhere, but not there.

Still, we managed to see each other outside of school and, while we never had much sex, we shared a wonderful sense of connection – a sense that we should be allowed to be together, and that somehow nothing could go wrong as long as we *were* together. I think some of my close friends knew about him, but it was never discussed. Similarly, we could occasionally hang out together, but we knew we always had to be discreet. We could hang out, but we couldn't touch if others were around. When others had playful back-and-forth interactions as teenage lovers do, we knew these things were forbidden for us. I suppose it was all part of the classic, "I like gay people as long as they don't insist on public displays" attitude, which is really just a variation on, "Don't ask, don't tell." If you happened to do or to say anything that someone else took the wrong way, you could be accused of "telling" or "displaying," and then you were in trouble. Big trouble.

* * *

The first time I had actual sex with a man I was 15, and it was with Charles. I suppose it was very Canadian, seeing as we thrashed about in a snowbank.

I went to visit Charles, who lived with his brother in a cabin quite far from the rest of civilization. While we had never discussed sexuality, Charles and I had a very close bond. He was three years older than I was, which can sometimes seem vast at that age, but it didn't to us.

We decided rather late one night to go for a walk in the snowy moonlight. For those who might think of snow as being frigid, I need to point out that on this part of Vancouver Island snow was a fairly rare thing. It never got terrifically deep and it didn't last more than a few days. Later, when I moved to Montreal, I learned that snow could fall frequently and be brutal, and that at least a foot of it could remain hard on the ground from mid-November to early April. Not so in the Cowichan Valley.

Anyway, we went for a walk. As we were enjoying the moonlight and each other's company, Charles looked at me and said, "Well, are we going to do anything or not?" I was blissfully naïve and didn't quite know what he meant, but he grabbed my crotch, led me to the snowbank at the side of the road, and proceeded to show me in rather glorious detail exactly what he meant.

It was not the "best" sex in terms of finesse or anything of that nature, but it was wonderful and real and a bit messy and quite lovely. We kissed a lot and felt each other (all over) and took turns exploring one another. I don't know how long it all lasted. We walked back to the cabin holding hands (until we reached the door) and never dropped a hint to his brother.

Our relationship went up and down for the next several years, and we didn't see a lot of each other. When we did, though, we always managed to find some time and space for a least a bit of quick and secretive sex. We never discussed it with his brother – although at some point he had to have put two and two together and come up with five. We were not the most discreet, especially if a bottle or two of wine was involved.

* * *

Charles was my only gay sex partner until I moved to Montreal, though it wasn't really for lack of trying. I would certainly have considered other partners had the opportunity presented itself, but it never seemed to. Probably a good thing, too, in the end – although at times I felt I must be very unlovable. Everyone I knew was having a lot of sex (with people of the opposite gender, mind you) and I was not. Oh well. That's the way it goes, I supposed.

* * *

I had a friend who, like me, was a student at the University of Victoria and a candidate for ministry in the United Church of Canada. She and I got into a very heated conversation about homosexuality one night at a party. She made no bones about the fact that she thought it was wrong, a sin, and something that should render one not only unfit to be a minister, but unfit to call oneself Christian as well. I didn't have a lot of arguments to offer by way of defence. Several times, I meekly tried to interject "Yeah, but …" into the conversation, to no avail.

I was, therefore, intrigued when she later got quite drunk and consequently quite friendly with another fellow at the party, and they went off to another room to be by themselves.

Hmm. It was wrong for me to be gay, but not wrong for her to sleep with someone? I didn't raise the issue with her, but I filed it away for further contemplation. Until that point, I had somehow believed that the Bible was quite black and white on things like sexuality, but now I wondered if maybe that wasn't the case.

* * *

I took some solace in the church, even though it was slim comfort because you could not be gay within the church in those days, either. But it was a place of support for me otherwise, and a place where I could continue to explore the spiritual parts of my life, which was necessary.

I also sank into depression – hardly surprising when you live a life you can't ever talk about. Three things kept me going. One was the music of Leonard Cohen who, I'll grant you, was never the cheeriest of singers, but especially not in his early years. His songs spoke loudly to me, and I felt a kindred spirit in them even though he was quite blatantly heterosexual. It didn't matter; what was important was that he put into song a lot of the things I was feeling.

The second thing that kept me going was the music of Miriam Therese Winter and the Medical Mission Sisters. The music was simple – one could even say overly simplistic– but again the words were new and fresh and honest. I also appreciated that, as time went on, MT (as I later learned she liked to be called) rewrote a lot of her songs, taking out the blatantly sexist lyrics of the earliest incarnations. I guess I liked that her faith journey was evolving, as was my own. I had the wonderful opportunity to meet her and spend some time with her when I was in my 30s and going through another difficult patch, and it was so wonderful to learn from her about how she had coped, and about how I could cope, too.

The third thing was simply my faith in God. I knew that there was a God who loved me unconditionally, even though life could feel lousy sometimes. Okay, a lot of the time. But still, God was there — present in the background even when it was coldest and stormiest and scariest. Somehow, I remembered that I was loved and accepted by this God, no matter what. And I always would be. Always. Knowing this kept me alive when I'm not sure anything else would have worked.

* * *

I remember going to a gay bar for the first time. It was in Victoria, and I was 18, just under the drinking age. By this point I had been drinking in bars since I was 14 and thanked my fairly mature looks for helping me to pass as much older. In any event, I mustered up massive amounts of courage and went to the Queen's Head.

I was pretty naïve. I didn't know anything about bar life in general, and I had no idea that most gays didn't go to bars until much later in the evening, so I showed up around 7 p.m. The door was unlocked and I stepped into a dark and silent space. There was one man behind the bar putting glasses away. He looked up at me.

"Hi, honey" (yup, he called me "honey"). "Can I help you?"

"I ... I'm here for a drink," I stammered.

"Oh, we don't open until 9. But you be sure to come back

then – this place gets pretty wild." He went back to putting glasses away and I left quietly.

My heart was pounding and I was thoroughly embarrassed. In retrospect, I shouldn't have been, and I'm sure the bartender forgot me soon afterwards, but I was seriously mortified. Yet there was something very tantalizing about going to a bar full of gay men that was going to get "pretty wild," so I went home, changed all my clothes (in a completely idiotic hope that the bartender wouldn't remember me) and went back at 9:15. And it *was* wild. Crazy. Exhilarating. And terrifying – all rolled into one.

I stayed for a couple hours and actually managed to dance with one guy. Otherwise, I sat at a table taking in all the noise, drinking copious amounts of beer, and wondering what it all meant. I remember leaving, walking home, and thinking that this was *not* my scene.

Then I remember waking up the next day and thinking, "You know, that was cool." Even so, I didn't go back for over a year.

* * *

I was really very naïve when it came to men. I think that helped keep me alive later on, because otherwise I would have undoubtedly been eager to go anywhere with anyone and do anything, and that, as we all came to find out in the early 1980s, was what could get you killed.

I look back now and think of a number of men who were putting the make on me – or at least trying to – and I was simply oblivious. I could probably have had an ample amount of sex in my late teens except that I didn't catch on. One fellow sat beside me for hours, as close as we could be without actually doing anything, and rubbed his leg against mine, and breathed on my neck several times, and I just got drunker and drunker and didn't think anything of it.

I had yet to fine tune my "gaydar," and I also had yet to realize that just because a guy had a girlfriend it didn't necessarily mean he wasn't gay. Not if you just wanted to have some harmless fun, right?

Like I said, my naïveté probably helped keep me alive and so it wasn't a bad thing all in all. Except that I missed out on a lot.

* * *

There were some moments in the 1970s when I came close to being outed, or was actually outed. Being outed is when *someone else* proclaims that you are gay. It's usually not done with a malicious intent – although it certainly can be. Often, someone just lets something slip and the word is out, there on the floor, in front of everyone – rarely like a beautiful blossom, but more often than not like something the cat just coughed up.

One time, I was home from university for a visit and was at a gathering. I was standing with a group of people that included several friends and my mother. There might have been others there as well, but I don't remember – I was too devastated by a fleeting moment of conversation.

In the midst of some banter, a friend said, "You know, Donald's bisexual."

Okay, he said bisexual – that wasn't quite as bad as saying "Donald's gay," but geesh, it was close. And in front of my mum! While I was soaring through a few nanoseconds of gut-wrenching panic, he followed it up with, "Yeah, he can do it with people on both coasts."

Everyone laughed.

Even me. Kind of. Barely. A bit. A forced little thing.

I wanted to kill him. It was just too close to the bone. But, of course, I never said anything. And, after some time had passed,

I secretly wanted to thank him because, in the strangest of ways, perhaps he had made it easier for me.

Another time, someone was talking to an adult friend of mine and mentioned that I was gay.

The other woman responded, "Doesn't matter to me. Donald is a person."

I held on to that one for dear life.

* * *

On the other hand, there was the time I went to a youth weekend at a United Church camp. I was a teenager and a lot of us were finding a bit of a renaissance within the church. We could keep things hip and cool, and within that found a place to belong.

It seemed comfortable. For someone like me, it seemed safe.

I remember sitting with one boy who I thought was cute. I never told him that, of course. I don't think I even did anything that intimated it. But he also might have picked up on it anyway, for any number of reasons. We sort of connected, and in the midst of things I told him I was gay. Boy, was that dumb.

He acted as if it didn't matter, but a while later when we were all having lunch (there were probably about 25 of us at this camp) a couple people came over to me.

"Darrell says you told him you're gay. Are you?" The question could hardly have been more accusatory.

"Well, I, um … " (I looked up, I looked down, I tried to look anywhere – but it didn't work.)

"Yeah," I breathed out with a heavy sigh. "I am."

"You know that's against the Bible, right?" one girl said. "Like you could go to hell for that."

"Yeah," chimed in another. "A man shall not lie with a man as he lies with a woman – it is an abomination."

"I don't even know how you can call yourself Christian," another boy said. He looked me up and down with the most hateful disgust. I wanted to die – really.

I. Wanted. To. Die.

Darrell – the boy I had first told – came over. "What's going on?" he asked. I don't know why he asked – it seemed pretty obvious that he knew what the conversation was about.

Without getting an answer, he simply said, "Leave him alone, guys." As if they were relieved to have an exit strategy, the others all left.

"Thanks," I said, with relief.

"Don't talk to me, faggot," Darrell said and walked away.

Given the wilderness location of the camp – combined with the fact that I was not about to phone my parents and say, "Some of the kids here found out I'm a screaming queen, so could you come and pick me up?" – I had no choice but to stay until camp ended the next day. It was without question the longest and in many ways most frightening 24 hours of my life to that point.

The group that had challenged me got larger, or at least it seemed that way, and they loved to give me dirty looks when I appeared. There were a few others who I can only assume were oblivious to what had gone on who would still talk to me. But it felt like I had no place there anymore. I did not belong. Perhaps I would never belong.

* * *

Some might wonder how, or why, I hung on to my faith. At a quick glance, it seemed that the church at that time was on a mission to stamp out people like me. Except that it wasn't *all* bad. Let me be clear: in the '70s I didn't find a single person who was about to say, "the church is a loving place where anyone, regardless of their sexuality, can be a welcomed and beloved part." Yet I still experienced a sense of unconditional love in many circles and, beyond that, I really felt that somehow things would change. They had to.

I realized it was a little like the many times when I and other Protestants smugly wanted to say to Roman Catholic progressives, "Gee, your church is so horrible and repressive, why don't you just leave?" Usually, when we did that, the response was, "No, it's *my* church, and just because it's led by a bunch of conservative old men with outdated theology doesn't mean I'm going to leave. I'm not going to let them kick me out of *my* church." Over time, I came to understand that.

Somehow, it had become instilled in me that there was some kind of inevitable progress to civilization; that despite setbacks we were on a trajectory that would always become more loving, more just, more open, and more accepting. So I felt that I had a place. I also knew that I wouldn't go back to a church camp for a long time, if ever.

* * *

At some point in the 1970s I met Martha. She was the mother of one of my best friends. She was divorced, and we all thought she was pretty hip. Lots of us loved to hang out at her place, where visiting always happened in the old living room she had turned into her bedroom. She spent the bulk of the day sitting in bed (dressed, I hasten to add) and we could all smoke and talk about deep and profound things. It was cool to be allowed to smoke and swear in the presence of a parent — something that was *never* an option at home

I never felt a particular attraction to her or that we had a relationship other than she was my friend's mother, and that was hip and cool. There was nothing sexual between us, and so it became quite comfortable to joke about sex and sexuality with her. That was cool, too, because that was another thing you generally couldn't do at home — at least not with the same mixture of vulgarity and bravado that spiced the conversations at her place.

Probably I should have seen it coming, but I didn't. I was blindsided and left in a very uncomfortable and vulnerable spot when she proposed that she and I have sex.

* * *

It happened after I had moved to Victoria to attend university and was living on my own. She somehow made the leap that I wanted to have sex with her. Later, when I tried to pull away, she tried to convince me that it had all been my idea. It took me years to realize it was a lie.

The thought had truly never crossed my mind prior to her invitation. I mean, come on — I was 18 and she was 50-plus. Really? At the same time, the thought of having sex with *anyone* had the appeal you might expect for any other male my age.

Sure.

Why not.

And so we began to have sex. While I saw it as little more than an occasional release, for Martha it was clearly more. She invested our relationship with something that, to her, was powerful and sacred. She would talk about how we were destined by God to be together, and that I must not fight it. She said I needed to give in. And besides, she could cure me from being gay, and didn't I want to lead a normal life?

Well, I didn't mind playing along because I was, after all, 18 and horny. And, if she could give me some kind of "normal" life (whatever that meant) maybe it was worth a shot.

* * *

Things became creepy early on. Martha let me know that I owed her this relationship because it was our destiny, and she argued that it would be wrong of me to talk about it to anyone else, or to sleep with anyone else. Years later, I began to see this as classic perpetrator nonsense, the kind of thing many abusers say to ensnare their prey and keep them subservient and beholden.

***

Martha was keen to emphasize that I was really good in bed. In truth, I doubt that I was, having had virtually no experience prior to that point. (But hey, it sure boosted my ego.) She emphasized that her plan to fix me of my homosexual tendencies was progressing nicely, and that this was a good thing for my future.

Her tactics didn't work.

As I came to full, sexually mature flower, as one inevitably does as you reach the end your teens, I did so as a gay man. I couldn't deny it and I couldn't fight it. I was who I was. But I continued to sleep with Martha and would then be overcome with guilt. Initially, I didn't understand the guilt or know what to do with it, so it became overwhelming. Slowly, though, I realized I was betraying myself. That realization in turn felt very confusing because part of me thought there was something wrong with me for even thinking that I was gay. Yet at the same time part of me knew that was okay. Confusion ruled the day – and Martha and I went on having sex. Lots of sex.

And I kept feeling worse and worse about it all.

***

I have tried many times to make sense of the whole Martha affair. I wanted to let her off the hook, to say that I asked for it because I made sexual jokes all the time, and that I was indirectly and inadvertently putting the make on her. It was very hard for me to accept that this was an older woman taking advantage of a younger man, pure and simple. There was nothing holy, or sacred, or mystical about it all. It was just sex, and while part of me enjoyed it, a larger part feared it and loathed it. She was older than my mother. She should have known better.

* * *

It was because of Martha that I knew I had to leave – or at least she played a significant part in that decision. I had to leave if I was going to have a life. I could not be who she wanted me to be, any more than I could have sprouted wings and flown, or grown a third arm. Somehow, though, she thought if we just had enough sex that could actually happen.

Bullshit.

* * *

For many years, she wrote me long letters – 22 pages, twice a week. She had discovered that she could write that many pages and still mail the letter for one stamp (the pages were not large). I read the first few with interest, and saved them, too. Then I began to read them and toss them. Then, I would skim them and toss them. Finally, I wouldn't even open them, I would just toss them. Little did I know at the time that this was a sign of some serious healing on my part.

* * *

At the time, though, I just knew that I needed to get as far away as possible and while St. John's, Newfoundland, would have provided that option and still allowed me to stay in Canada, Montreal seemed far enough. When I got accepted to McGill University, I ran or, more precisely, flew on the first jet I could find.

My parents were sorry to see me go, as were many of my friends, and most of all Martha. But I knew I had to do it.

While my choice of Montreal might suggest that I wanted to hide, in fact I wanted exactly the opposite. I wanted to be somewhere where I *didn't* have to hide, where I could be *me*, and not have to worry about who might see me.

In that sense, I wasn't just moving *to* Montreal, I was also moving *away* — away from a town that was just too small. The small fishing and pulp mill community on Vancouver Island in which I had grown up had, like most small towns, tried its best. I mean, really small towns usually have the best of intentions. But they are intentions based on the assumption that everyone will fit. There isn't much room for odd-shaped pieces in the jigsaw puzzle of small-town life. If at some point you discover that you are an odd-shaped piece, one that doesn't fit, you really have only two choices: you can either try several very painful ways to shave off the edges that make you different (even though there isn't any place where you will ever really fit), or you can leave.

* * *

The choice to move to a big city was a good one. Montreal offered a different culture and different language, and with the Parti Quebecois freshly in power in the late '70s things were happening and changing. I wanted to be there and to be a part of it all. Montreal was also very old, with vast houses built a one or two hundred years ago — some even 300 years ago — out of huge blocks of stone — something you never saw in western Canada. At the same time that it was old, it was also very new, with skyscrapers and an underground Metro system, and noisy streets, and French signs everywhere.

Best of all, virtually no one knew me (I had one friend when I first arrived) and so it felt much safer.

* * *

At that time, Montreal was more tolerant of people who didn't quite fit into the norm. Or at least so it seemed. Its intolerance towards people of other races, ethnicities, and cultures has always been a black pot sitting on the back of the stove — sometimes more quietly than at other times, but always simmering and ready to boil over at a moment's notice.

When I arrived, even though I was an anglophone from western Canada, the fact that I was excited about speaking French and fitting in earned me a reasonable amount of acceptance. And the fact that I was gay? It earned me the odd yawn. It seemed to be a non-issue. Most of the time at least.

* * *

While moving to a big city was a good choice, continuing to live and work within the framework of the Christian church could have been seen, and *was* by some at least, as odd. Yet the seminary I chose (United Theological College) offered an interesting array of classes in progressive things, including a class on Gandhi, who was a hero of mine.

As seminaries go, United Theological was quite different. The Quebec education system was structured in such a way that the seminary could not teach academics, only practical stuff. This meant that we took our academic classes at McGill University (across the road), and then did a finishing year of practical theology at the seminary proper. But our college social life centred around the seminary, which was contained in an old house that provided a wonderful atmosphere and a supportive environment.

As I look back on it some 40 years later, I think it was probably the safest seminary to be attending in those days for someone like me. That is not to say that everyone was open and supportive, but the overall feeling was "we won't kick you out because of who you are – no matter who you are." Recently, I was talking to a friend about life back in the 1980s, and about the seminary in general, and she agreed with me that it was probably the best and safest place to be in those days. Certainly, it was one of the most progressive seminaries on the continent at the time.

She also pointed out – and this is key, I think – that there was both a right-wing church and a left-wing church, and they were both the same church. It's not as if we could draw a line and say, "these denominations are liberal ..." and "these denominations are conservative ... " because the meaning of those terms was increasingly fluid. But within the church, even though technically there was a formal, accepted theology that hovered over everything, there were also those who were keen to break the rules, or at least to challenge them.

As my friend put it, "The church could be as wrong as the best of them, yet there were those who would shelter within themselves little germs of justice and reconciliation and compassion." That kept a lot of us going.

***

In Montreal I finished a degree in comparative religion with an emphasis on Jewish studies. I really don't remember a lot of the material I studied for that degree because part of me just wanted it to be over so I could pursue ministry. However, I did begin reading the Bible in earnest, or at least in more serious ways than I had before. And I began to encounter people who had thoughts and questions about religious matters, which was not something I was used to. Where I grew up, conversations about theological and philosophical matters were as rare as they were vague. At McGill, such conversations were frequent, more serious, and required more interaction.

I also befriended some folks at the seminary and by the grace of God fell in with a liberal crowd. The seminary was not large; there were about 30 students at any given time who were part of its program of study or affiliated with it. I connected with a small handful of pretty radical folks who liked a good drink, or to smoke a little pot, and to talk about how our ideas were going to change the world. We were keen to put down more conservative people and believed that we were always right. It helped that the seminary administration was very liberal at the time, and so we felt we had pretty free reign.

It was jarring, then, to encounter anyone – either from our seminary or from one of the other seminaries affiliated with McGill – who was extremely right-wing, and in turn encounter theologies that were far less compatible with who I was and what I was thinking. In the latter part of the 1970s, the dual debates about the place of women in the church and the place of gays in the church blustered, with a lot of wind and smoke swirling around them. I was a little taken aback.

While there had not been many female ministers where I had grown up, there were at least a few, and so the idea of women in ministry seemed pretty normal to me. I could not understand why, at the end of the '70s, this was still an issue for anyone. More controversial than that, though, was the issue of gays in the church. It seemed that as the church came to grips (at least nominally) with the idea that women were or should be perfectly equal to men in the life of the church, many wanted to draw a line there. One couldn't let this all get out of hand now, could one. The church was letting the women have a place – better to stop there for a while.

Consequently, it was not uncommon to encounter people

who had readily memorized the handful of verses (no, really, there are just a handful in the entire Bible) that seemed to condemn homosexuality, and who bandied them about with varying degrees of enthusiasm and/or vitriol, depending on their point of view. I couldn't understand – and I still cannot understand – how people can claim Christianity, a faith base on unconditional love for all people, and yet take an almost orgasmic satisfaction in finding a few verses in the Bible that seem to exclude others.

In the face of this, I – like many others in the LGBTQ+ community – felt helpless. It seemed there was nothing that could be done about those few verses. But it nagged at me, and when things nag at me, I can't let them go.

* * *

I tried to do all the research I could on those pesky verses, and a couple things emerged. First, I discovered that the Sodom and Gomorrah story – which was a favourite of those who wished to exclude gays – wasn't about homosexuality at all as it turned out, but about being inhospitable. One of the worst things you could do in ancient Jewish society was to turn away or not welcome a stranger, to be inhospitable, which is exactly what is happening in Genesis 19. And, interestingly, every other time the story is referred to in the Bible (except one) it is used in the context of inhospitality. How ironic that a story that condemns us for not being welcoming was, and too often still is, used to support and encourage unwelcoming and inhospitable behaviours!

I looked into the meaning of other verses and phrases, as well. "Lying with a man as with a woman" was condemned as an abomination, but as I learned in Hebrew class "abomination" did not mean "horrible sin that will condemn you to the fires of hell for eternity plus a week" but rather "something disgusting." There's a big difference. Something may be "disgusting," but that does not make it a sin. I discovered that references in the New Testament were even vaguer, and that biblical translators (those who translated the Hebrew and Greek texts into English) often had to take a "best educated guess" at what certain words meant, especially if those words only appeared once in the Bible. Some translations actually said "homosexual" when the Hebrew or Greek word referred to child abuse and pedophilia – neither of which are related to homosexuality.

Beyond those few references, something else happened. I found stories that seemed to affirm being gay and, in my mind, these began to trump the few obscure verses that could be interpreted to say the opposite. They also allowed me to move away from arguments with people over what an obscure Greek or Hebrew word might have meant several thousand years ago and to focus instead on the overall message of scripture and the words of Jesus. Wow! What an eye opener!

* * *

My favourite biblical story became the one about the fellow from Ethiopia who encountered the disciple Philip while riding home from Jerusalem; it's in Acts 8:26–40.

The man is a eunuch, which is an interesting term. It could mean that he was born with deformed (or no) male genitalia, or that he had at some time in his life experienced a tragic accident that left him disabled in that area. It is possible he had been castrated, which was not an uncommon practice in those days for men who worked closely with women. However, this was seldom applied to men of high rank, and this man was the minister of finance. Or it could also mean that, because he worked for a woman (the Queen of Ethiopia) others simply called him a eunuch, kind of like people today might call a man who works for a female boss a wimp or a wuss.

The thing is, according to the Hebrew scriptures, a eunuch cannot be part of the faith community. They are excluded, kept out, banned, forbidden – choose the word that works for you, but notice that it doesn't really matter; they cannot belong. They are kept outside. And it had something to do with their genitalia. As someone who was often told I could not belong because of something regarding my genitals – specifically, what I might occasionally do with them – that story and that insight spoke to the depths of my heart.

According to the story, the fellow from Ethiopia is intrigued with Judaism and so he travels all the way to Jerusalem to worship at the temple – even though when he gets there, as a foreign non-Jew with a bad name (*eunuch* was one of those words that would have repulsed people) he would not have been able to enter the temple itself, but only stand outside.

He happens to pick up a copy of the prophet Isaiah while he's there and on the way home he is reading it. Along comes the disciple Philip, just as the Ethiopian comes to the part where it says,

Like a sheep he was led to the slaughter
    and like a lamb before its shearer is silent
    so he didn't open his mouth.
In his humiliation justice was taken away from him.
    Who can tell the story of his descendants
        because his life was taken from the earth?

"So," asks Philip, "whatcha reading?"

"The latest from Isaiah," the Ethiopian says, "although I can't really understand it. I can't tell if he's talking about himself or someone else; it doesn't make much sense."

Philip seizes the opportunity and says, "I happen to be familiar with that story. If you give me a ride down the road, we can talk about it."

The chariot stops, Philip hops in, and proceeds to tell the man about Jesus. None of us can know the exact details of what Philip said, but I'm guessing it was a story about love for others, and about risking everything – even your life – to proclaim the message of God's unconditional and everlasting love for *all* people. You know, the message that Jesus taught over and over again, and was killed for.

The man is so excited to hear a story that obviously includes him he asks if he can be baptized. Without any hesitation, they stop the chariot by a puddle, hop out, and the man is baptized, included in the family of God – despite the fact that he's a foreigner, and not Jewish, and there's a problem with his, you know, crotch. And then Philip disappears.

I read this story. And I read it again. And I read it *again*. Each time I read it, it spoke to me in ways that were transformative. This was my "ticket" – not to eternal life or anything like that, but a ticket that told me, in black and white, what I had been feeling since I was a child. God loved me, I was included, and you could do your worst. I belonged. Oh boy, everything was going to be okay now.

Or not.

* * *

At the same time as I was having this epiphany, I continued to run into folks who would say something along the lines of "Gee, I'd really like to accept you and all, but I just can't go against scripture." It was when I read Matthew's version of the birth story of Jesus (Matthew 1:18–25) for the umpteenth time that I found some help with this particular attack.

When Joseph finds out that Mary, his fiancée, is pregnant, he knows that the baby is not his. We are also told that Joseph is a "righteous man," which means he knew the Jewish law, especially the parts that he might have some "contact" with. This in turn meant that he would know Deuteronomy 22:20–21, which deals with a young woman being found to have had sex with a man to whom she is not married: "If the claim is true and proof of the young woman's virginity can't be produced, then the city's elders will bring the young woman to the door of her father's house. The citizens of that city must stone her until she dies because she acted so sinfully in Israel by having extramarital sex while still in her father's house. Remove such evil from your community!"

Well, that was pretty clear, pretty black and white. She's pregnant and isn't married? Kill her. Sounds straightforward to me. Except ...

Except Joseph has a heart. He can't do this. I mean, he's probably really ticked off with Mary for getting pregnant, but kill her? He's not quite *that* mean. So he decides, instead, to put her away quietly, as some translations word it, which basically means send her away to a neighbouring town where no one will know the circumstances, and she can have the baby and live. In that scenario, he probably wouldn't have had anything more to do with her, but she would not be killed, let alone in such a brutal fashion.

As I read this passage, and then read it again, I was struck by a key piece. Joseph let compassion and concern for another human being outweigh scripture. He knew the law, he knew the rules, and he blatantly chose to disregard them. What's more, God basically commends him for it, telling him to go ahead and marry her and to live happily ever after. God is not the least bit upset in this story that Joseph made the choice to disregard scripture; in fact, God, via the angel, requests it.

If that passage can be right there in the Bible, why do people think they can hide behind scripture in order to tell me – and others like me – that I don't have a right to exist, at least not within the wonders of the Christian church? I couldn't let this one go.

* * *

At my seminary each fall they held a series of lectures funded and named for a major benefactor. One year while I was there the speaker was William Sloane Coffin, a renowned U.S. theologian who at that point was senior minister at the huge Riverside Church in New York City.

Riverside is an intriguing entity. The building stands huge, defiant, and majestic, overlooking the Hudson River in Morningside Heights. It was primarily funded by John D. Rockefeller and opened in 1930. The first preacher was Harry Emerson Fosdick. For its time — and arguably ever since — it has stood at the forefront of liberal theology and has attracted some pretty serious preachers to serve as its senior minister.

I was eager to hear Coffin when he came to McGill. He had earned a lot of respect not just among people in the liberal church, but arguably with some of the more mainline Christians and denominations as well. And he was generally known as one of the best speakers and preachers around.

He spoke in the afternoon, and then again after supper. As he ended his afternoon remarks, he said, "Be sure to come back this evening. I'm going to talk about abortion and homosexuality."

I went to supper with my friend Todd and expressed my excitement that the great William Sloane Coffin was going to talk about homosexuals in the church. Todd was less than enthused.

"I'm always nervous," he said, "when someone who's straight wants to talk about the big 'H.' I worry about how they're going to present things."

I understood where he was coming from, but at the same

time I thought, hey, this is William Sloane Coffin. What can go wrong?

He spoke about abortion first, and the need for the church to be less hardline – on both sides of the issue – to exercise more compassion and more understanding. Then he turned to the topic of homosexuality.

I don't remember much of what he said, until the moment when he closed. He looked up from his notes and said, "Why does the church want to throw away your gifts just because of who you sleep with? It doesn't make sense." He paused, then shook his head. "It just doesn't make any sense."

In the microsecond of silence between his last word and the applause that erupted in the room, I felt a wonderful, warm glow – someone important, who was not gay, had just expressed what I had felt for so long.

It has *never* made any sense to me that the church wants to cast off the amazing gifts of thousands of people just because its uncomfortable with their sexuality. No sense at all.

* * *

The 1980s had begun with my time in seminary. By the end of the '80s, I was an ordained minister living in the United States. In between, AIDS happened. Okay, it didn't *happen*, as such. It was more like it crept in quietly – at first – and slowly began to take over life in the LGBTQ+ community. People caught it and died from it. People tried to avoid it and still caught it and died from it. Some people caught it and miraculously lived with it, although in those days, for the most part, AIDS equalled a death sentence.

* * *

I woke up in an isolation ward. I was too sick at the time to know what that really meant, except that whenever anyone came to see me, they had to stop in a little room outside – I could see them through the glass – where they would don a gown and gloves (the fancy type of gown that fastened at the wrist, not some loose thing), and a mask, before coming in.

When they left, they had to reverse the process, and include rigorous hand washing with some industrial-style soap. (This was before the days when we used hand sanitizer like it was water.)

I didn't know I was that infectious. Of course, I wasn't – but no one knew that in those days.

We didn't know *anything*, really. The doctors and nurses, and certainly the journalists and newscasters, were just shooting in the dark. Sleeping with someone could kill you. Kissing someone could kill you. Touching someone could kill you. Looking at someone sideways could kill you. Allowing someone to live and breathe could kill you.

If you were gay, you lived in fear. You knew very little, but you *did* know more than the straight population – you had to. Or at least you had to pretend you did, because you wanted to be seen as keeping on top of the latest news about that thing that could take away the life you knew in a heartbeat, in a quick few minutes in an alley or a bedroom.

You knew more because, at any point, someone – a doctor or a well-meaning friend – might ask you about T-cells and blood counts, and things you didn't think you would have to ponder until you were at least in your 50s or 60s. But now, thinking about living that long seemed a strange luxury. Really? Weren't we all supposed to imagine growing old? Wasn't it part of our DNA, or at least our birthright as people in the developed world?

You had to know more because you knew someone who died too young – at age 22 you had been to funerals of friends, something even your parents didn't do with as much frequency. You had to know more because you knew someone who had mysterious symptoms that no one could figure out. Or someone who tried frantically to deny that their flu was anything more than that. Or someone who had strange blotches on their skin that they covered with too much makeup, trying to pretend they didn't have Kaposi's sarcoma so they wouldn't get fired. Or someone who went from living in a beautiful condo with a view and a great job to living in a studio bedsit while collecting welfare and relying on someone to bring them groceries every week – which seemed a little pointless because their appetite had disappeared, either because it was actually gone or because consuming cocktails of pills that didn't do any good had taken it away.

It shouldn't have been like that.

It should *never* have been like that.

No group of people should have to deal with a pandemic on their own, and yet it happens too often. The difference, I think, was that most other times it happened far away, in other countries on other continents, and we could let the racism we grew up with insulate us from reality. This time, though, it was here. It was us.

* * *

My mother's on the phone.

I'm in the hospital thousands of kilometres away from her. She knows I'm sick. Very sick. And she knows I'm gay. I hear the terror in her question.

"Donald," she pauses, long enough for me to know what she's going to ask, but maybe she didn't mean it that way. Maybe she just didn't want to ask, because questions lead to answers. Not asking questions means we can live in ignorance. Or die in it.

"Donald, what about AIDS? Is it AIDS?"

No parent should have to think that kind of question let alone have to ask it of their child. Yet I am so grateful now that she could ask it then, so we could get it behind us.

* * *

There was a whole alphabet soup of letters in the early days — in part, I am sure, because no one really knew what it was. Or maybe it was so that the realities could be hidden behind letters that would tell those who had a right to know what it was all about but could be passed over by those who did not want to know.

GRID – Gay-Related Immune Deficiency This was one of the first terms. Except there were lots of people showing the same symptoms who weren't gay, but they tended to live in places like Haiti and Africa, so we could ignore them. When it began to effect hemophiliacs and others who maybe got infected blood via a transfusion, this name fell into disuse rather quickly.

AIDS – Acquired Immune Deficiency Syndrome The catch-all name that meant a death sentence for some, fear for others, and was a source for great anger and loud screams of "told you so" and "serves you right," for still others. (In some circles it was referred to as Acquired Immune Deficiency Disorder, although the initials AIDS remained the same.) While a syndrome is theoretically just a cluster of symptoms, over time it became synonymous with "disease."

ARC – AIDS-Related Complex, for those who were going to get sick and die but who hadn't quite hit the worst of the downward slope. Yet.

HIV – Human Immunodeficiency Virus. In the early days, we would never have heard of let alone been able to pronounce or spell a word like immunodeficiency or have known what it meant. But when more and more people began catching *something* yet didn't seem to be hurtling towards death as quickly as others, this became the preferred term. By the time it arrived the concept was already far too familiar.

* * *

Danny was the first of my friends to be diagnosed.

I was living in upstate New York by this time. He phoned me from Montreal and said, "I've got it."

I didn't have to ask what *it* meant. I knew. We all knew. It was too familiar, too frightening a thing for us not to know what *it* was.

"I've got it."

I was silent for a while. What could I say?

He was 21.

It was 1983.

He was going to die.

* * *

It was a photographer who alerted Danny to the possibility that he was sick. Before he was aware of having any symptoms, he was doing a photoshoot, trying to launch a career as a model. One of the poses involved him dressed in nothing but a pair of tight jeans, standing on a boat, looking out to the horizon.

"You've got something on your back," the photographer had said. Danny tried to turn his head so he could see it, but it didn't quite work.

"It's okay," the photographer said, "we can airbrush it out. But you might want to get it looked at."

Danny hadn't even heard the words Kaposi's sarcoma before.

* * *

Danny came from Alberta.

His parents were conservative.

His dad worked in the oil industry and his mother did all the proper and appropriate things to support his career. I never met them. Sometimes I convinced myself that they were probably nice people who loved their son as best they could and prayed at least once a day that he would change, that he would grow out of it, that he would just meet the right girl so everything would be perfect. At other times I thought they were just uncaring assholes.

He was their only son. He had a sister who was a few years older, who was married and lived in Calgary. Same neighbourhood as the parents. Her husband worked in the oil industry, too. I can picture them sharing drinks and dinner of an evening, the grandchildren swimming in the pool in the backyard.

If only Danny could have played by the same rules, followed the same patterns, done the family proud, everything would have been fine. But he couldn't. And it wasn't.

*　*　*

Danny's parents would say, always trying to keep the proverbial stiff upper lip, that Danny was not the marrying kind, that Danny was a little bit different, that Danny was an artist, that Danny had moved to Montreal. (Somehow living amongst the French could explain why none of us were married.)

Danny had told his parents he was gay, but only after he was safely several thousand kilometres across the country. I can't blame him; I did the same.

But really, did any of them *not* know? I mean, deep down? Really? Despite all the euphemisms and the false hopes (you study too hard – you should get out and meet some girls) it should never have been a surprise.

We were queer. We liked watching musicals and we memorized the songs. We were far more interested in going to the art gallery than going fishing. We put a lot of energy into trying not to pass bitchy and catty comments about everything going on in the world around us, and we had to make sure we didn't use the wrong pronouns and say "she" when referring to a friend, or an effeminate man on TV.

* * *

Sometimes we would use the same lines that others used, but we would use them with our tongues firmly in our cheeks. Sometimes we'd use a female pronoun, but we were always talking about a man:

She putts from the rough.

She's a shirt lifter.

She's got a little sugar in her tank.

She's walking down the other side of the street.

She's part of the family.

She's on the team.

Knowing the incredible enthusiasm the gay community had for the film *The Wizard of Oz* and the wonders of discovering at some point in your life that you were no longer in Kansas, eventually we in the LGBTQ+ community landed on calling ourselves "Friends of Dorothy" – sometimes abbreviated to FOD. This carried a little more mystique, was slightly more removed from simple reality. If someone shot a disparaging glance, you could shrug your shoulders and say, "It's just an expression. It doesn't mean anything." Bullshit. No one ever bought that. But it was a lie you could hide behind until you could quietly slip away.

* * *

Obviously, part of being gay in the 1980s was secrecy. It was paramount. Gone were the days – okay, *mostly* gone were the days – when you could get arrested for being gay, for standing on the wrong street and looking the wrong way. But it was still dangerous. People lost jobs – often. You could lose your apartment, even when you had a lease; you'd be amazed how quickly those could disappear when the landlord discovered you'd had a male friend spend the night in your one-bed apartment.

Certain professions had no room for us at all. Gay schoolteachers? Too risky. Gay men in jobs traditionally connected with testosterone (engineer, logger, millworker, truck driver)? Too risky.

The military? No, without question.

Religious leadership? You're kidding, right?

It was bad enough if you were gay. It was doubly or triply bad, or even worse, if you were suspected of having, you know, "*it*."

* * *

My symptoms began with what felt like flu. Except that this time the flu wouldn't go away. It lingered for weeks. I saw the doctor several times, but he just said, "Go home and rest. Drink plenty of fluids. If you get really bad, go to the emergency room."

One day my temperature hit 40 degrees Celsius (104 Fahrenheit). I was delirious. Some people came to see me and when I didn't answer the door they walked into the house. I was sitting in the living room (apparently; I cannot remember) talking to someone who wasn't there. They decided to take to me to the hospital.

"They" were people from my church – a United Methodist congregation in upstate New York. How I came to be there is another story, which I'll get to later. For now, though, I simply point out that "they" were from the church because I wonder now what they thought. This was the early 1980s, and the thought of a gay minister in a small town in upstate New York was unheard of. Right?

Yet there had always been rumours that I was, well, let's just politely say "questionable."

So what did they think? It was November. People got the flu. They even got other things that were worse, but they didn't get AIDS. Not people you knew. Not people who had respectable jobs. Not people who, well, now, come to think of it, we were getting to the point where you didn't have to think that way anymore. Stories were becoming more frequent in the paper about this strange illness that was hitting a wider range of people than had first been thought. You didn't have to wear really tight pants, lisp, and have a hint of eye shadow. You didn't have to be a hairdresser or own a poodle. It could affect anyone.

They took me to the hospital. Did they wonder? A little, or a lot, or not at all because, after all, I was the minister?

They took me to the hospital and dropped me off at emergency. I recall a nurse helping me into a wheelchair. And then I lapsed in and out of consciousness for several hours.

* * *

Danny and I met for lunch a few days after he phoned to tell me of his diagnosis. I got there first. When he walked in, I thought I could sense weakness and fear. Was it real, or was I projecting those things onto him now that I knew?

He wore a large scarf, which seemed a bit odd. Montreal is known for its freezing winters, but this was April, when we usually celebrated the coming warmth and wore as little as we could get away with as a show of defiance.

Danny came to the table and removed his jacket. Then he

looked around before he removed the scarf. I saw two brownish-purple lesions – each about the size of a quarter. Had I not known he was sick I might have thought they were hickies and made some rude comment, but I had read enough and heard enough to know that Kaposi's sarcoma (a skin cancer previously confined rather strangely to Jewish and Italian men in their 50s) manifested exactly this way.

As if sensing my thoughts or perhaps noticing that I was staring, even if only for a second before turning to look him in the eye, Danny offered in a whisper, "That's Kaposi's sarcoma. It's the telltale sign that there's no turning back. I'm dying."

What was strange was that he said it with a weird mix of defeat and relief as if – and I've heard this from other men as well – he knew he would catch it some time, and so there was something reassuring that he didn't have to wonder anymore. How sad, I thought. And yet how real.

We ordered. I had already told him I would pay – seemed like I had to do *something* for a friend who was dying.

A friend who was dying.

Those were words I wasn't ready to put into a sentence. Maybe in another 60 years, but not now. Not for someone who was only 21.

"How have your folks taken it?" I asked.

Danny's parents were Pentecostals. There was no room in their faith for someone as far from the norm as Danny, for someone who was gay. Maybe if he had lamented it and begged to be "healed" there would have been room, but not for someone who said, "This is who I am."

Certainly, there was no room in their minds for someone with AIDS, certainly no words in their vocabulary to say matter-of-factly, "Our son has AIDS." As I said earlier, I have usually tried to believe they meant well, but I also knew that deep in their hearts they believed being gay was a sin, and that somehow AIDS was God's statement to the world that this was so. No matter that other people died of AIDS, not just gay men. No matter that this was nonsense because God does not work that way. No matter that this was their son – a fact that ought to trump everything else.

"I haven't told them," Danny said.

"Really? You've got to tell them. I mean … " I paused because I knew there wasn't really any truth to what I was about to say, but I said it anyway, "they're your parents."

What did that mean, exactly? Years ago, they provided one egg and one sperm and Danny was the result. Over the years they celebrated his first steps and read him stories and took him camping and loved him.

Now he was dying of a "sinful" disease. Did that suddenly cancel everything out?

"Yeah, I know … I'll have to tell them," Danny said. "But how, you know? My mum's going to cry, and my dad's going to yell and then go silent. God, I hate his fucking silence. He does it whenever he doesn't know what to say and I just can't stand it." Danny paused. "I just can't stand it … " The words trickled away, lost in the thought that it didn't really matter, because when you're dying you have to tell your folks. I mean, you can have a cold, or a hangover, or an STD and they don't ever have to know. But this was different. Danny was on a journey with one destination.

We talked about a mutual friend. I knew Danny and Todd had slept together, but I knew it had only been once, and I never did get any details on what actually transpired.

"Do you think he's got it?" I asked worriedly.

"No, I don't think so, but he's already gone for a test. Gets the results soon, I think. I'm pretty sure he doesn't have it, though. I mean, we didn't do anything that could have … " I didn't need the rest of that sentence because I knew what he was trying to say. Todd was safe. The thought faded away into a mix of hope, fear, and anxiety. Was it okay to express relief over one friend's near miss with death while talking to another friend who was dying?

* * *

"He'll find out soon," Danny repeated, this time a little more hopefully.

Wow. What would that feel like, to think that you might have inadvertently given it to someone? To think that you might have – inadvertently – killed someone? I shuddered inside.

"But your folks, man – I mean, don't get me wrong, I can't imagine telling my parents. They'd freak out (pause). But still, you're going to have to do it. Do you think you can do it on the phone, or would you go back to Calgary?"

"I *will* tell them. And it'll have to be on the phone; I can't afford to go to Calgary. I can't afford much of anything. Benoit said he'd take care of the funeral."

Oh. My. God.

* * *

At some point prior to all this, Danny had met a man named Benoit. I cannot remember how they met, although I'm sure Danny told me. I'm guessing it started with an encounter in a bar and escalated from there.

Benoit was older – not quite old enough to be Danny's father, but he probably had close to 20 years on Danny. He could fulfill that kind of father image, which I think Danny craved. And he had the wherewithal to look out for him.

Because Benoit worked for one of the airlines, he could get free tickets, and he and Danny travelled to a number of places:

New York, Paris, Florida. It was a world that Danny loved and, while he still hung out at the bars and picked up men on a regular basis, he and Benoit had a kind of relationship. I think it broke Benoit's heart, frankly, that Danny slept around so much, because Benoit struck me as the kind of man who wanted the "normal" life of a monogamous couple, and spending cozy evenings curled up on the couch in front of a gentle fire, snuggling over cups of hot cocoa. That was not Danny – not by a long shot. Yet Benoit put up with him, gently welcoming him back to his home when Danny would venture there for a few days at a time. Danny kept his apartment as well, almost to the end, but he had a second home with Benoit.

* * *

A doctor told me once a few years back that I should lose a little weight. I laughed to myself. The doctor was correct, of course; I have always been a bit overweight. Never really obese, but I could always stand to drop at least ten kilos.

"Losing weight's always good," the doctor said. "It will add to your lifetime."

Will it? Yes, it will. Because I know it is my weight that probably helped keep me alive.

I was overweight just enough that I didn't fit in the overly cute column. No one looked at me and thought, "Okay, let's go to bed."

They might have looked at me and thought, "He's a possibility for later if he's still here in the bar after 2 a.m. and no one else has said yes." That's not very reassuring when you're in your early 20s and trying to meet someone, but it does mean that you don't have a lot of sex. And in the 1980s that was without a doubt the most dangerous thing – having a lot of sex.

It should not have been. I mean, I am not trying to encourage or promote promiscuity, but the simple reality is that you didn't have to be promiscuous, you just needed to have one experience with one infected person who had had one experience with one infected person …

It's not that gay sex is bad.

It's not that any kind of mutually agreed upon sex act is bad.

It's not that sex is bad.

It's just that it was the vehicle for sharing a virus that killed people. And the odds went up the more people you had sex with.

* * *

I woke up in an isolation room. A nurse was doing all that nurse-stuff they do when you first get admitted — writing on a chart and hooking me up to an IV bag of rehydrating solution.

"I'm going to put in a Heparin lock," she said slowly, as if I were too young to be very familiar with anything medical. And I was. Way too young. Mercifully young. Frighteningly young.

"That way, we can administer anything we need to without having to poke you again."

"Thanks," I thought. It was only later that I began to worry: What did they think they were going to have to give me? And the bigger question: What did they think was wrong with me?

* * *

Danny did tell his parents, and it went exactly as he had predicted. His mother had phoned him twice afterwards, but he hadn't spoken to his dad who was always "busy," she'd say apologetically when she'd call.

Busy.

Too busy to talk to a son he'd never see again.

Too busy to have a conversation with the son whom he had vested with so many of his own dreams and hopes.

Too busy to think about how that son had thrown all those dreams and hopes away. I mean, what right did Danny have to live his own life, to be true to himself? Didn't he know he owed his dad something? Didn't he know that his parents didn't have him just so he could go to bars and get laid every night? Didn't he know that he wasn't supposed to die, damn it?

***

Todd's mum "kind of adopted Danny," as Todd himself put it. She felt sick about how his parents had treated him, and she phoned Danny to say that she would be proud to call him her son.

Danny cried whenever he thought of that. In that simple act she had spoken volumes and done something amazing – she had told someone he belonged. Someone who should have known that from his own parents who, for any number of narrow-minded reasons, were incapable of offering him the unconditional love that all parents owe their children. Yet when they could not tell him he was loved, a stranger came to the rescue and reminded him of that fact.

As I've talked to others over the years, I've heard this has happened a lot. People who have been abandoned by their parents have found love and acceptance elsewhere. How horrible to have to look for that when you're dying.

***

I only visited Danny a couple times in the hospital. I probably could have gone more often – he was there for about six weeks – but it felt too strange. Not the hospital part, but the reality that he might not leave that place. That it was over – we knew that it was over – but he was still putting in time. It seemed such a horrible thought.

* * *

One time when I did visit Danny at the hospital, we just sat in silence for a while. It seemed as though there wasn't really anything to say. I attempted some small talk – noticed something outside the window I could make a banal comment about, wondered how the food was (stupid question – his thrush was so bad he hadn't eaten anything in at least a day). But for much of the time we just sat in silence.

At one point I looked at Danny, kind of thinking he might be asleep, and saw him on the verge of tears. It took me by surprise.

"I don't think about dying much," he said.

I grunted or offered some meaningless one-word response.

"I guess I should. I mean, in my head I know it's going to happen. They told me I've got like one to two months left before *something* kills me." He paused. Catching his breath, perhaps, or just catching his thoughts.

"I'm not scared of it either," he said. "But I'm scared of dying alone." He reached out and squeezed my hand – hard. "That's what I'm scared of. I mean, I know I can't ask you or Todd or anybody to be here all the time – I'm not asking you to, Schmidtty. But I'm scared of being here all alone, and then not being here, you know?"

"You won't die alone," I said, after a very long pause. I said it, even though I had no idea why I said it. How did I know? I mean, if I thought about it, I would have realized the odds were that he would, in fact, die alone.

"Yes, I will," he said. "I know I will." He paused. "I guess it's okay. I mean, there's nothing I can do about it. But it scares me, you know? Just to think there's not going to be anyone holding my hand."

"I know," I said. "Like, if you were married there'd be ... " I let the thought die off. It was so silly. Of course he couldn't be married, because he wasn't straight. Of course he couldn't be married, because that was only an option for a man and a woman.

In those days, hospital visiting hours were quite strictly enforced. They'd make exceptions for people who were dying to have an "appropriate" loved one with them until the end. You could always have your wife or your husband there, around the clock if you wanted.

But not if you were gay. Not if you were dying of AIDS. Then you suffered alone. Underneath that little reality lay the assumption most people held: somehow you had brought this on yourself. You deserved it. And even in death you would pay.

You would pay by dying alone. It was your lot.

Danny managed a soft, quiet smile.

"It's okay. I know it will happen that way. You don't have to beat yourself up over it. It's not going to be your fault."

His demeanor changed, and a certain anger came into his voice. Weak though he was, he managed an angry sort of growl.

"Of course my mom won't be here. They won't even come to see me now. I'm dying, for Christ's sake. They're never going to see me again. Never. And they won't come. Nor my fucking sister." Now he was overwhelmed with anger. His voice cracked as he burst into a horrible coughing fit.

"I hope they go to hell," he said.

I scrambled in my thoughts for some theological wisdom to share but came up with nothing.

"You don't really mean that," I offered, realizing as I said the words how pathetic and pointless they sounded.

"Yes, I do! I *do* mean it! They can go to hell! Think about it,

Schmidtty; I'm their only son." He coughed again. "I'm their only son and I'm dying, and they can afford it – they could fly here first class and not even notice the expense. They could come here for just one day – just one fucking day and hold my hand and tell me they loved me. But they won't. They say they can't, but I know the truth – they won't. They just won't, because having to accept a son dying of AIDS isn't in their picture of the world. And *that's* why I'm going to die alone. Even if you and Todd and everyone from school was here, I'll *still* die alone."

I looked away so he wouldn't see me start to cry. He turned away, too, I can only assume for the same reason.

A moment later he seemed to be asleep. I wondered afterwards if he really was asleep, or if he just wanted me to think it so I'd leave, because there really was nothing more to say. Nothing at all. The horrible truth had been set out in plain air, and there was nothing more to be done.

I squeezed his hand – he kind of squeezed back – and I left.

* * *

As it happened, that was the last time I saw Danny. He rallied, a bit, and actually got to go "home" to Benoit's for the last few weeks. He even grew strong enough to venture out for very short periods, now and then.

He was blessed, in the end, to have a home to go to. Benoit provided that for the time Danny had left. Benoit provided a place for Danny to die, with a hint of dignity and some comfort at the last.

* * *

Todd was at home when Benoit phoned him to tell him about Danny. He drove over right away and was there in about ten minutes. Danny was sitting up in bed, sort of slouched over but, for a split second, he looked good enough that Todd thought he hadn't died yet. Of course, he had, and Benoit's tears underscored it.

Todd struggled being there. Danny was the first person any of us knew who died of AIDS. But it wasn't just that. Todd had had a big blow out argument with Danny just a few days before.

There was a book sale at McGill university and Danny really wanted to go and get some books. Todd took him because there was no way Danny could have walked the few blocks from the subway to the student union building where the sale was being held. As it turned out, they had trouble finding parking and so Todd had to drop Danny off near the door and leave him to wait for what, to Danny, seemed like an eternity while Todd found a parking spot. When Todd got to the door, Danny asked him what had taken so long and Todd almost yelled at him, but didn't.

They looked at the display, and Danny kept picking up more and more books. Todd was carrying them and, after a while, thought they had more than enough, but Danny kept looking, and grabbing more books.

Finally, Todd had had it. "This is enough, Danny," he said.

"But I want some more. I have nothing to do but read these days."

Todd blew up. "For Christ's sake, Danny, you'll be dead before you can read all of these."

Of course, he regretted it as soon as the words escaped his lips, but it was too late. Far too late.

Danny simply walked to the door. He probably would have left, but he didn't have the strength, so he slumped down to sit on a chair by the exit. Todd picked up the books, bought them all, and walked over to Danny.

"Here," he said, handing Danny the books.

Danny waited while Todd went to get the car. When Todd

got back to the door to pick Danny up, he noticed that he didn't have the books. He was going to ask what had happened, but Danny guessed it and spoke first.

"You were right. I'll never have time to read them before I die."

Todd felt horrible, and they drove back to Benoit's in near silence. A few days later, Danny was dead.

* * *

Todd called to tell me that Danny had died. We cried on the phone. We talked about the funeral; Danny had asked Paul and me to do it, and it was held at the school chapel.

We weren't sure how much the school would charge us to use the chapel, and in turn weren't sure how we would pay for it, until Benoit said he would cover all the costs. As it turned out, the school didn't charge us anything. They knew that Danny had no money, and that Todd and I didn't have much, either.

It was the first AIDS funeral to be held there, but it was hardly the last. I attended probably close to half a dozen in that space over the next few years, and there would be many more besides.

The chapel was on the second floor of the Faculty of Religious Studies. While it was ostensibly an interfaith chapel, it was built to replicate a rather classical Church of England monstrosity, with stained glass windows and a pipe organ, and kneelers in each pew. Everything about it screamed "proper" and "English" and "Christian" and "stiff upper lip." Sometime afterwards, we managed to laugh at the fact that Danny's service was attended primarily by guys he knew from the various gay bars he frequented, and most of them looked – and no doubt felt – extremely out of place. Yet they were there, out of respect for their friend.

I read a bit of Shelley's "Adonais" at the funeral.

Peace, peace! He is not dead, he doth not sleep —
He hath awakened from the dream of life —
'Tis we, who lost in stormy visions, keep
With phantoms an unprofitable strife,
And in mad trance, strike with our spirit's knife
Invulnerable nothings. — We decay
Like corpses in a charnel; fear and grief
Convulse us and consume us day by day,
And cold hopes swarm like worms within our living clay.

I had first encountered the poem when Mick Jagger read it at a memorial for Brian Jones back in the 1960s and, while I didn't really understand it at the time, it spoke to some part of me. Over time I have returned to it when I think of Danny and others who died from AIDS.

Shelley wrote it when he first heard of the death of John Keats at age 26 from tuberculosis. Key for Shelley was the sense that Keats would no longer be subject to critics of his work, and I couldn't help finding parallels to Danny and others who have been challenged by the world at large for simply being who they were — nothing more, nothing less. For their mere identity they were ridiculed (at best), despised (more often), and generally cast onto some heap of nothingness. But they were people. They were boys — rarely old enough to be called men in the truest sense of the word, and had a right to exist, to flourish.

They had a right to simply be.

Like a poet criticized by those who simply didn't understand good poetry, Danny and others were too often criticized by those who didn't understand that people have a right to exist, to simply live their lives.

* * *

I was struck by something Danny had said to me the last time I visited him in the hospital before he died. He was looking away, out the window.

"The thing is," he said, and he turned to look at me. "The thing is, I just wanted to be loved. That's all."

* * *

The thing I remember most about Danny's funeral was the lavish bouquet his parents sent. It was obvious they could have flown to Montreal — money was no real object for them — but to do so would have meant admitting that their son was part of a world that they really didn't want to know, that they really didn't want to get involved with.

So they sent flowers.

The bouquet from Danny's parents ended up at Benoit's apartment after the service. Several of us were standing around with drinks and nibblies. Someone walked over to the bouquet, took out a handful of flowers, tossed them on the floor, and stepped on them.

"That's for never coming to visit your son once when he was in the hospital," he said in a voice that was significantly louder than he might have used had he not had several glasses of wine.

His action unleashed a flood of emotions for all of us there, and people began to take other flowers from that bouquet, and then from the other bouquets, and stomped on them, making statements about a world that seemed not to give a damn about the boys and young men who were dying because they slept with the wrong person.

How were you supposed to know who was the wrong person?

"That's for all you straight fucks who think we deserve it," shouted one person as he dumped the rest of the bouquet, flowers and water and greenery, on the floor. The rest of us fell silent for a moment. It seemed so harsh, so loud.

It seemed so real, and so true.

Too true, we would learn as time went on.

* * *

The phone would ring.

"I've got *'It,'*" someone would say.

As always, there was no need to define *It*. We all knew what *It* meant. *It* meant AIDS.

We knew that it was out there; we knew that it was elusive and mysterious and vague. And we knew that, without intervention, it would get us all in the end.

* * *

Just the ring of the phone triggered fear for some.

To answer the phone, just to pick it up, risked bad news. If you didn't answer, the news couldn't hurt you, right? Ignorance was, if not really bliss, well, at least it could buy you time. Because truth, truth could kill you.

Maybe it was someone saying they had *It*.

Maybe it was a friend telling you about another one, another friend, who had died, or was in the hospital – which meant they would die soon.

Maybe it was a doctor's office saying, "We'd like to see you." They wouldn't say that if it wasn't serious, right? If it was something innocuous, they would tell you over the phone, wouldn't they? When they wanted to see you – that could only mean one thing.

* * *

As the decade advanced, people started using condoms, but in the early years condoms were frowned upon.

I remember a fellow asking me once, circa 1982, if I ever used condoms when I had sex with guys.

I shot him a snotty look and said, "Haven't you heard? They've determined that men can't get pregnant."

"Yeah, but there's a lot of bad stuff out there. It's worse than before. There's *really* bad stuff – here, and in San Francisco, and in New York, and you want to be careful."

To the best of my knowledge that was the first conversation I ever had with someone about safe sex. And I tried to pass it off as a joke.

* * *

The thing is, it's not about sex.

I mean, it is, but it isn't.

Sex is good and it's fun and it's a wonderful part of life.

Yet for many gay men the pursuit wasn't just for sex, it was for *someone*. It was for someone to love, and to be loved *by*, as Danny had said. Even though we enjoyed the sex and wanted it, and sought it, I think the vast majority wanted something more. We wanted to be loved. We wanted to have a relationship with someone. We wanted to hold someone in our arms and have them look into our eyes.

We wanted to come home to another man, and make plans with another man, and laugh with another man, and have fights with another man, and make up afterwards with another man.

Is that so much to ask?

Did it have to be so complicated?

We would often talk about this in the '80s, and I've thought about it a lot since – that the goal, the dream, was to fall in love. Whether one was going to be monogamous or not was seldom the issue. The issue for most was first and foremost about finding someone to love.

Is there anything wrong with that?

* * *

I went to Halifax along with some other students from my seminary, to attend the Canadian Theological Students' Conference in 1980. It was an intriguing conference, bringing together a variety of students from across the country and from across the spectrum of the Canadian church; there were Roman Catholics, Presbyterians, Baptists, Lutherans, Anglicans, United Church people, and a smattering of folks from more obscure denominations.

Several of us were gay and we discovered early on that Halifax had only one gay bar. The first evening we all headed over there. It became our regular haunt for the three or four days of the conference.

On Sunday, due to Nova Scotia's strict liquor laws, the bar could not serve alcohol, so they opened as a "coffee house." The significance of this was that young people could go, and so there were quite a few teenagers there. Oh how I wished there might have been something like that when I was younger! A place to go and hang out with other gays and lesbians in a safe environment where you could be among your "own kind."

Someone who worked at the bar asked Todd and me if we could talk about what we were doing in town. We shifted from one foot to the other and suggested we didn't really have anything to say. Being a person in training for religious leadership did not rank very highly among folks in the LGBTQ+ community. Or so we thought.

"We know you're here for something relating to the church," the fellow went on. "We'd love to hear what you have to say about the place of gays in the church today."

Todd and I stammered, then shared a bit about our understanding of church and the community. We also invited questions and were amazed by the volume of questions folks had, and by the overall interest of the entire group. There were probably 40 or 50 people there that day and they listened to us for a good half hour. I was impressed.

When we were finished, the fellow who had asked us to speak came up to us. His words hit me hard, but in a positive way.

"I'd like to thank these prophets," he said, "for coming here and reminding us that there is a place for us in the Christian church." And people clapped.

They clapped.

In a gay bar.

It was an awesome experience. In many ways, it was a watershed for me. In the years following, when I would wonder whether I really belonged or not, I would think of that day. I had been called a "prophet" and I had told others that there was indeed a place for them in the church. I guess I needed to believe it, too.

* * *

There were several Roman Catholic priests and priests-in-training at the event, some of whom were also gay. I had a question burning within me and, once I was suitably lubricated by several beers, approached a few of them and asked, "So I don't get it. I mean, how can you be gay and celibate? Doesn't being gay mean you have sex with men? You don't have sex, so how can you be gay?"

One of them offered a simple response that caught me off guard.

"I'm not celibate," he replied, and walked away.

Another offered a more meaningful answer. "I chose celibacy because it is a part of my calling to be a priest. I chose not to enter into a sexual relationship with another person, and to devote myself entirely to serving God. But if I were to be sexually active, it would be with a man."

Prior to that day, I mostly hadn't thought of it that way. For the most part, I had equated my gender and sexual orientation with sexual activity. But as I reflected on this man's answer I realized more and more that being gay meant more than who I wanted to have sex with. It was about who I was, about how I viewed the world, and about how I lived in the world.

* * *

Eric was a young man whose life intertwined with mine when I lived several years later on Maui. He was 19 and I was by then around 50. He lived on the street and he was heavily into drugs.

I met him on the street and through conversation ended up inviting him to stay at my place. He ended up staying for a few months.

Eric's story was tragic. He had been out of his parents' house since he was about 12, having been shifted through programs and psychiatric hospitals and foster homes. I don't think there was anything really wrong with him, except that he didn't fit the mould at home and they needed to make him fit into at least *some* mould.

Someone told me Eric was gay. It didn't really surprise me. He was pretty, if a little worn around the edges from too much time without a place to call home. I could understand someone having a sexual interest in him.

But I was not one of those people. Eric was young, and I was much older, and the relationship was only ever a pseudo father-son kind of thing. I told him I would be proud to consider him my son, and he appreciated that, even though we knew he wasn't.

Eric had HIV. I knew this when he moved in because he told me. I was okay with that, although I appreciated knowing so that I could be a bit more diligent. By this time – the 2000s – we knew more and did not panic the way we once had.

I asked Eric one day about being gay. He looked at me sheepishly.

"I'm not gay," he said.

"Really? You know I am, right? I mean, you know it's okay, right?"

He laughed. "Yeah. But no, I'm not gay." Deep breath. "It's just that I caught HIV from using drugs, from dirty needles. But if people find that out they look at you funny. If they think you got it from being gay and having sex with another guy it's way better. They feel sorry for you."

Wow.

Times had changed.

* * *

One of the strangest and most unpleasant things I've ever experienced was several hours in a refrigeration blanket.

Yup, it's as bad as it sounds.

My temperature by this point had reached 41.7 Celsius (107 Fahrenheit) and they had determined I was in serious danger. Life-threatening danger. So they put me in a refrigeration blanket.

It seemed strange to me. I had a terrible fever and thus I was shivering. You shiver when you are cold, so I assumed I must be super cold to be shivering as much as I was. And they wanted to put me in the fridge? Okay.

A refrigeration blanket is exactly what its name implies: two pieces of fabric with refrigeration coils between them. I'm sure the advertising brochure describes it much better than that, but they wrap it around you and turn it on and then you freeze for a while. It's literally like being in a fridge, and my learned opinion now is that this is the epitome of "what doesn't kill you makes you stronger."

But I really did think it might kill me.

Without question, I was the weakest I had ever been and didn't have a lot of stamina to call upon to get me out of the pit, and now they wanted to freeze me.

I don't know how cold the thing really got, but I know I was in it for several hours. I think they put me in it right after lunch, and I was in it through supper. Not that it mattered, because I really couldn't eat anything, I was too feverish. But the body knows mealtimes instinctively; it's how we know what time of day it is, or at least how we know we're still alive.

* * *

And then there was the Jewish doctor. Normally I would never name someone that way. I can never understand why people insist on naming a person's race or religion for no reason other than to indicate that the person is different from them.

But in this case this doctor's Jewishness was relevant. Actually, it was his watch. I had been out of it. As I came to, a doctor was looking at me, and his wristwatch was directly in front of my face. And it was in Hebrew.

I had never seen a Hebrew watch before, had never even known one existed before. But here it was, an inch or two from my eyes, with Hebrew letters where you might expect numbers or Roman numerals. Instinctively (because I had studied Hebrew in seminary) began to utter the letters aloud: *aleph, beit, gimel, dalet* ...

"The patient appears to be awake," the doctor noted.

This was when I noticed that a half dozen youthful and eager medical students, all equipped with the requisite flip chart and pen, were staring at me. And for good reason.

The sheets had been pulled back, and my handsome hospital gown was pulled back, and I was lying there naked. Of course, to the doctor and the eager students I wasn't a naked man; I was merely a specimen to observe and learn from. Suddenly the Hebrew watch paled in its significance.

"You will note the colour – a deep purple (I thought fleetingly of the rock band of the same name) that is already beginning to move."

Move? Colours move?

"I anticipate," the doctor continued, "that it will progressively move towards each of the limbs, and slowly abandon the body through the toes and fingers. The colour will remain as dark, if not darker, but the torso will return to its normal colour as the rash moves away."

Interesting.

"There are several things that could cause this rash. One of them is a pulmonary embolism, but we can rule that out, I think. Another possibility is a cardiac arrest – the patient *did* exhibit slight signs of that yesterday."

I did? Nobody told me. Must have been when I was out of it. Maybe somebody *did* tell me and I don't remember. Am I losing my mind? I suppose it's possible. They say that a serious temperature can cause brain damage. Great.

"What we think is most likely, however, is Henoch-Schonlein purpura, or HSP. This is an inflammation of the blood vessels that we believe is caused by a malfunction of the immune system." He paused for the students to write this down, which they did very properly and importantly.

"Could you spell that for us, Sir?" one of them asked.

The doctor did, then continued: "The patient has also exhibited substantial diarrhea – we've got him on medication for that. But this rash is very interesting." He pulled my gown back down over my torso and, most importantly for me, my crotch. (Thanks, doc.) "We'll discuss this more later. Now, moving on to our next patient …" and the doctor ushered the students from the room.

Okay, so now I knew a few things. First, I was just "the patient" – didn't get so much as a "good morning" out of this guy, and the students just looked at my torso – or my dick – the whole time.

Second, I had a purple rash. I raised my head – a difficult task as I was still incredibly weak – lifted my gown and looked. Oh my God! I really *was* purple. I mean, seriously purple, like a ripe eggplant.

Third, what was that about the immune system?

* * *

I only had sex with Jack once.

He had stopped by my house while he was in town – he and his wife lived a few hours away, but her mom lived near me and they would come to visit her occasionally. I was surprised when he stopped by because I had only met him once before, at lunch with a mutual friend.

"I was going to go to the rest area," he said, "but then I remember you lived nearby and thought I'd stop in."

That told me immediately why he was there. The local rest area on the highway was a renowned spot for gay men to pick up someone for quick sex – casual, nameless and, if it was dark enough out in the trees where you might go to do things, even faceless.

But he had chosen to visit me rather than go to the rest area.

I suppose I should have seen it as a great compliment, but instead I just took it for what it was – a simple statement that he had not come for polite conversation. I was the lucky winner who got to join him.

"My wife is at the mall. I told her I would only be a little while." In other words, let's go upstairs and get down to business.

I had never been like that, where sex was just a simple transaction between two people designed to get at least one of them to orgasm as quickly as possible. For me there was always at least the fantasy of a commitment, of some mutuality, or at least of wanting to please the other person and enjoy the moment. But I soon realized that for many gay men – and especially for ones who were married and needed to scurry around furtively – it was exactly what I experienced that day with Jack: quick, albeit enjoyable, with no strings attached.

I knew that Jack loved his wife, and that probably they would have had a great relationship were it not for this one glaring thing – he was gay, and she was a woman.

We had sex. I can say it was enjoyable, but it was also pretty quick. It didn't last long.

I never saw him again. He died from AIDS within the year. I only slept with Jack once.

* * *

I tried to imagine Jack telling his wife. I can't imagine it, really. How do you say something like, "Honey I'm attracted to men. And I've been having sex with men behind your back. And now, because of that, I'm dying. Oh, and can you care for me until I die? I don't think it will be too long."

* * *

Jack had trouble coming to grips with the fact that he had AIDS. This was understandable, seeing as he was an officer in the Salvation Army. It was difficult enough for those of us in the "mainline" church, but I couldn't begin to imagine what it must have been like to be gay in an organization such as the Salvation Army. No wonder he chose to keep things secret.

Years ago, Geoff, my boyfriend at the time, was reading something that the Salvation Army had published that said there were no gays or lesbians in the organization. He wrote them a letter pointing out that he knew of quite a few and would be glad to provide names. He never heard back.

**

Jack told his wife, and others, that he must have contracted some kind of virus when they had lived in the Caribbean years before. We heard the story and of course did not believe it. It was just too obvious that Jack had AIDS; he slept around, was never careful, and it was frankly only a matter of time before he contracted it.

But this was still an era that forced gay men to tell other stories, and so he lived behind a thin façade of some kind of respectability. I can only imagine what it was like the day he learned his diagnosis from the doctor. Had he been surprised? Or had he, like so many others, simply recognized and accepted the inevitable?

Incredible as it seemed to the rest of us, Jack's wife seemed to accept his story at face value, and she patiently cared for him at home while he died. The symptoms were those of AIDS, but he kept the ruse going. It was only years later that Sandy admitted quietly to someone, almost as if testing the waters to see if the world would blow up, that the illness Jack had had might have been AIDS. It was perhaps the closest she ever came – or that any of us ever saw – to accepting the reality of Jack's life and death.

I never knew if she was aware that Jack was gay. Sometimes I think she must have known. Except I know that denial is a strong thing for some folks.

I talked to Geoff about it, because Jack was much more his friend than mine. "I doubt that they ever discussed it," Geoff said. "I'm certain she knew. But it was never discussed. I've talked to Sandy several times and it's never come up in the conversation. Jack comes up in the conversation, and the fact that he died so quickly after such a horrible virus had attacked him. But as to what the virus was, she's never said anything. Nothing. It's like she knew, but if she didn't say anything then she could hold on tight to some fantasy that he really wasn't gay."

"Of course," Geoff continued, "she knew he loved her. He really did. It's just that he needed others, too."

* * *

I was released from the hospital on a Sunday. I remember it very clearly because they told me several times that I was to see my regular doctor first thing Monday morning. They had arranged the appointment already. Eight o'clock. Don't miss it. It's very important. Do you want me to write it down?

Monday.

8 a.m.

It would have been nice if someone could have told me why, but there you go. I knew better than to ask questions.

* * *

"It's cytomegalovirus," the doctor said. "CMV. And you know what that means."

Nope—not the foggiest. What, you think I'm a doctor? God, this man could be irritating.

"No," I said politely, "I'm sorry; I don't know what it means."

"It means ..." he drew a breath, perhaps for courage, perhaps for dramatic effect, "it means you have AIDS."

The air got thick and blurry and mystical. For a microsecond, time seemed suspended.

"I'll be right back; I'll give you a moment to think about that," he said.

He left.

And I did think about it. I had three thoughts in fairly rapid succession.

The first, *fuck!* AIDS? Really? Oh my God. I'm going to die.

The second thought was very different and shows you how my mind works when I have to process things that are difficult — it jumps to something completely unrelated and completely ludicrous. (It's an ADHD thing, apparently.)

I knew that the doctor had lived in this town all his life and I wondered how many women he'd looked at? In the stirrups for an internal exam. I started thinking of women in my parish and wondered if he'd done their exams.

It was a horrible thought, to be sure, and frankly it's difficult 40 years later to admit it with all its layers of sexism and inappropriateness, but sometimes we don't control where our brain goes.

The third thought was this, as I became filled with anger aimed squarely at the doctor: You've just told me I have AIDS, that I'm going to die, and then you leave the fucking room?

There's gotta be some scissors in here, a needle or two, or maybe a scalpel. There's got to be *something* I can kill myself with. It would serve you right — you tell me I'm dying and then you leave me alone. Thanks. Thanks a lot.

***

The doctor came back to the examining room with a file folder and some papers.

"So here's the thing," he said as if he hadn't just told a 24-year-old man that he had AIDS. "You don't appear to actually *have* AIDS."

So … wait … what? … huh?

I'm dying. I'm not dying? You told me I was dying just so you could have the fun of telling me that I'm *not* dying?

You left the room. You *left* the room, left me here *alone*.

You left me here to think about my own death, and then you come back and announce that I'm *not* dying?

"I don't understand … " I managed to say.

I could have killed him. Even though the news was good, I could have killed him. Don't do that. Don't do that to anyone, ever. Don't tell a patient they're dying and then tell them they're not. Like, did you change your mind? Did you just get a lightning bolt from heaven when you left the room? Is this some weird sense of humour thing, and now you're going to tell me again that I really *am* dying after all and that it serves me right?

"So, here's the thing," he said again. "All of your blood tests come back negative for AIDS. I'd like to run one more just to be sure, but we've done three quite recently and they all agree. It's very strange, you see, because while some people get CMV without contracting AIDS, given your situation we just assumed, and so that was our approach. But it appears to be different."

The bastard sounded almost disappointed.

I was furious with this man except I was brought up with a fierce sense of needing to give appropriate obeisance to those who were more learned than me, and so I felt I had to respect him and couldn't just run out and slam the door.

"So, I have cyto … CMV (thank God for abbreviations),

and usually people get that when they have AIDS, but I don't have AIDS? Is that what you're telling me?"

"Basically, yes."

I struggled to get enough strength to ask the next question carefully, and politely, and kindly – even though that isn't at all how I felt like responding.

"I'm wondering, then" (take a deep breath, focus), "why you told me just a minute ago that I *did* have AIDS? I don't understand?"

He didn't seem to breathe at all, just carried on as if we were talking about a cough.

"As I said, given your lifestyle (quick: how did he know? I thought I had been pretty discreet) it seemed to make sense, especially with the temperature you had, and with the CMV. You've also had thrush, which is another key symptom of AIDS. But while one blood test could give a false negative, two probably wouldn't. Three really cannot. And as I said, I'd like to run another just to be sure."

"Just because you think I'm a nasty, dirty little faggot, and you were convinced that it was only a matter of time before I dragged my sorry, disease-ridden ass in here and admitted that I was a terrible person and deserved to die, you thought you could have a little bit of fun and tell me I'm dying just so you could see the look on my face?"

That's what I wanted to say. Oh, how I wanted to say that, with all my heart.

"Okay," I said.

"Great. Here's the form. Just take it to the girls at the desk and they'll take care of things."

I was thinking clearly enough to wince slightly at the use of the word "girls" to describe grown, professional women who had the serious misfortune to work for this dickhead.

I took the paper and left.

***

The drive home from the doctor's office required great concentration. Not because I was trying to process the information and the experience but because I was still quite weak. I should have had someone drive me home, but I wasn't sure who to call. Also, after ten days in the hospital, I *needed* to drive myself because I needed to do something normal, something everyday. I had to do a simple, ordinary task that told me I was alive.

***

One of the worst things must be having to come out when you're dying. I can't imagine it, but I know of too many people who had to tell their parents in some sort of awful and convoluted sentence, "I'm dying. I'm gay."

I remember learning that Bruce had to tell his parents when he called to ask if he could move back home. He'd left home a few years earlier to go to university, and then dropped out and got a job at a gay bar. Now he was calling them to tell them one more thing. He told me he wanted to do it on the phone because he was afraid to do it face-to-face in case they rejected him, something he couldn't have handled, given the state he was in.

Imagine it. You're dying and your biggest fear is not death, or the process of withering away, but of your parents rejecting you.

"I'll never know," he said to me, "whether they were more shocked that I had AIDS or that I was gay. I think it was being gay."

***

The whole idea, let alone the experience, of having to come out to your parents is horrible, really, when you think about it. No one else has to do it. No black kid has to say, "Mom and Dad, I have something to tell you *(deep breath)*. I know you're white, and you always hoped I'd be white, too *(deep breath)*. But I'm not. I'm black."

What parents would kick their child out of the house for something like that? But for many gays it *was* and *is* different. They *did* and still do get kicked out of the house.

In order to be true to yourself, you do have to tell your parents, eventually – unless you're one of the fortunate few who had parents who raised the issue themselves, which can be embarrassing but at the same time spares you the agony and the fear.

I don't blame parents – for their initial reaction, at least. We live in a society that tells them, and the rest of us, that the "norm" is to grow up, marry someone of the opposite gender, and have the 2.7 children nature intended. When their kid says, "That's not going to happen" who can blame them for being taken aback?

But that's really all they should be allowed. I'm convinced that if they truly loved their kids they wouldn't say "Get out," or "No you're not," or even, "You'll grow out of it."

Because we won't. We know that, even if others don't. Even if we try to fight it with all we've got, deep down we know it's who we are. We cannot change it. My eyes will always be blue. My height will always be 5 foot 7. Even my hair, which is now changing from brown to grey, will only be the colour it wants to be. I can dye it, but the roots will always come back. Always. I'm not fooling anyone. I will always be gay. No amount of prayer or medication is going to change any of that.

* * *

I talked with Bruce shortly before he died. His mom was glad that I had stopped by and used it as an excuse to go out and run a few errands as long as I was there to keep Bruce company. By this time, I was serving the United Methodist Church. I bring that up only because Bruce's family, like so many who lived in that area, was staunchly Roman Catholic via centuries of family tradition. She gave me a slightly odd look and said, "You're the one who's the minister, is that right?"

"Yes," I said, a bit awkwardly because it seemed a strange question.

She paused. "That's nice," she offered, and left.

Bruce was glad to see me, and frankly I think gladder still to have his mother go out.

"She's driving me nuts!" he exclaimed. "I thought she'd be all judgmental and to be honest I kind of wish she was. Instead, it's all this 'you poor thing, you didn't know this disease was out there' crap. I got her good the other day, though."

He beamed with pride that he had gotten something over on his mother.

"What did you do?" I asked.

"Well, she kept asking me about how I thought I caught 'it' — she always calls AIDS 'it,' as if we're talking about some kind of living thing, a monster that's going to jump out from under the bed.

"Anyway, she wanted to know exactly how someone caught it. I was being vague, saying things like 'Well, it's from, you know, bodily fluids.' And she said, 'Well, what kind of bodily fluids?' I couldn't hold back anymore, so I told her *everything*. I mean, I told her about things I had done that I never even told *you* about."

Bruce had always taken great pains to describe his wildest nights in graphic detail, so I couldn't quite imagine the conversation with his mother.

"I told her what I did," he continued, "what I liked to do, some of the people I'd done it with. I told her about being gangbanged over at a party at the college, and about going to Montreal and hanging out at the tubs all night, doing every guy who came by." ("The tubs" was a slang term for what were more commonly referred to as "the baths" – places where gay men went to meet other men for sex. Ostensibly, there was a sauna and a hot tub and maybe even a pool, but really it was about having raw, anonymous sex – as much as you wanted, for as long as you wanted.)

"I thought I'd shock her, but she just seemed to take it all in. When I paused for breath, she just said, 'Oh,' patted my leg, and got up and left the room. I don't know what she really thought, although she hasn't asked me any more questions about how I got 'it'! And I swear, she gives me this funny look sometimes as if to say, 'Did you *really* do all that stuff or were you just pulling my leg?'" He paused, and then got serious for a moment.

"Like I'd tell her *any* of that stuff if it wasn't the honest truth. I mean, who tells their mother that kind of shit?" He paused again.

I thought, "Those of us who have nothing to lose I guess."

* * *

I have no intention of minimizing anyone's symptoms, but I have to say I think shame was the worst part, at least for most men. The sense of shame that they had somehow done something dirty, that they had betrayed their parents' trust, that they had stooped beneath anything their straight friends were doing.

That shame kept us from talking about it. It kept us hiding who we were, and what we were doing.

In the end it killed a lot of us.

* * *

I remember Danny insisting that he had caught AIDS from giving someone a blowjob. I know it's possible, although all the literature will tell you it's extremely rare. But he needed to hang on to this story. He said he couldn't bear to think people would look away from him in disgust and think "Serves him right – he got AIDS from anal sex."

* * *

It was always strange visiting Bruce. What was weird was having lots of questions but not daring to ask them. I mean, how intrusive must it be to be in your 20s, tell someone you're dying (because of sex) and then have them pepper you with personal questions?

I wanted to know what it felt like. Was there pain at the places where you had Kaposi's sarcoma? (No.) Do you worry if you're catching something else because of AIDS? (No.) Do you think about dying a lot? (Yes.) Did you know you would catch this? (Yes.) And the classic, "If you knew you were going to catch AIDS, what would you have done differently?"

Surprisingly, over time I heard different people offer answers to some of those questions (I'm proud to say I never asked them, even though I certainly wondered). Perhaps strangest of all, though, was the common, although not universal, statement that people would *not* have changed their behaviour. That answer seemed to change as time went on. In more recent years, I have heard people talk about wishing they had been more careful, and obviously a lot of people practice varying degrees of safe sex in ways that they didn't 40 years ago.

But it always surprised me that people would say, no, they wouldn't do anything differently. And then I realized that I didn't always protect myself, either. You get caught up in the moment and …

* * *

I remember being involved in a conversation with a renowned – and quite conservative – theologian, plus a third person with whom I went to seminary. The other fellow was concerned about having a gay son and thought the conservative theologian would support him in this – which he did, initially. However, as my friend kept going on about the need to convert his son, fix his son, save his son, the theologian interrupted him. I'll never forget it.

"You seem to be forgetting," he said slowly and intentionally, "that your first job as a parent is to love your child. Unconditionally. That's it. All this other stuff, it's secondary. You have to love them first, without any conditions and without any boundaries, and then you can think about everything else."

Later, he even went so far as to say, "I don't think homosexuals can change." He still didn't like us much, but at least it was a tacit acceptance that perhaps we were not all destined to hell. How can you be destined to hell for something you have no control over? Assuming you think there is a hell in the first place.

* * *

I didn't really come out to my parents; I came out to my sister. My initial plan was to tell her and, depending on her reaction – and any advice she might have offered me – I could decide how, or even if, to tell my parents.

I told her in a letter. In the midst of other things, I casually mentioned that I had been at a gathering of lesbians and gays and then said, "So I guess now you know the truth about your little brother."

I know she had guessed – I had hardly been the model of butch decorum when we were growing up. It was just the two of us growing up, and we were pretty close. She wasn't an idiot, and the signs were pretty obvious.

It was a bit shocking when I was talking to my parents a few weeks later and my mum said, "Your sister told us about your letter." The pause after that statement seemed to go on for hours and hours. "I think we're okay with that. It will take your dad a little longer. But I think he'll come around."

That's all anyone said about it for ages. I didn't want to say more, and neither did they. It wasn't until I took a boyfriend home from Montreal to meet them that they had to confront it.

When we came in the door, Dad said to Geoff, "Well … you could sleep with Donald, but we do have a guest room and I think you'd be more comfortable there."

Geoff commented afterward that he could tell from my dad's voice that he was really saying, "*I'd* be more comfortable. I'm still getting used to this. Don't rush me, please." Geoff slept in the guest room. It was okay.

* * *

I became part of a group that initially called itself "United Church Gays of Quebec" and shortly afterward expanded it to "United Church Gays and Lesbians of Quebec." We kept that name for a short while, until we discovered that you needed government permission to call yourselves anything with the word "Quebec" in the title, so we dropped that and, over time, morphed into the fledgling Affirm movement in the United Church. The bottom line was that we simply wanted a loose organization where we could meet and discuss common issues – and have a good social time as well.

There were quite a few of us, both ordained and on the path to ordination. There were a few lay people as well, although not many. We met every few weeks to discuss things, and then to have a party. I suspect that without the promise of the party we probably wouldn't have lasted more than one meeting.

One of the decisions we made was that we would no longer answer questions about sexual orientation when being interviewed for ordination. It wasn't relevant, in our view, and if it wasn't relevant, why would we play along?

We decided that the next person up for an interview with the committee would respectfully refuse to answer any questions that were posed about sexuality. We even did some role plays to practice what we might say and what it might feel like. They were good. Apparently, though, not good enough.

* * *

In those days, one of the things you had to undergo along the road to ordination in the United Church was a psychiatric exam. This meant filling in an instrument known as the Minnesota Multiphasic Personality Inventory (MMPI). I know that it has been revised several times since I had to fill it out, but at that point the church was using an instrument that had been developed in the 1930s and '40s. It did not take a brain surgeon to realize that the world had changed a little in the 40–50 years between the time the MMPI was devised and when I and the rest of my cohort were filling it in. No matter to the folks in the church.

A few of the questions on the form were crossed out. I don't remember exactly what all of them were, but I do remember one that was crossed out: "Are you sexually attracted to persons of the opposite sex?" Of course, they left the question "Are you sexually attracted to persons of the *same* sex?" untouched. In previous iterations of the test, before one of those two questions was crossed out, I knew people who had simply said "yes" to both questions. When questioned about their responses, they said that sexual attraction was a wide spectrum, etc., etc.

Perhaps it was to avoid this sort of conundrum that the screening committee crossed out one question and left the other in. It certainly showed a serious bias on the part of the committee, but that didn't seem to faze them.

I decided I simply would not answer the question, but that didn't get me very far. After filling in the form, I had an interview with a psychiatrist and sure enough she had a copy of the MMPI that I had completed.

"You didn't complete this question here," she said kindly.

"Yeah. I know." I shifted a little. "I just don't believe it's in any way relevant to the practice of ministry." I realized I was on shaky ground, because one could theoretically have argued the same thing about any of the questions on the form, from one standpoint or another.

"I have to put something down. We cannot use an incomplete survey," she said. I picked up on what I thought was a hint of apology in her voice, as if she didn't really agree with this practice of crossing out one question but leaving its opposite untouched.

"Put what you want," I said. To this day I'll never know what she did with that question, but that's where we left it.

* * *

As luck would have it, I was the next person scheduled for an interview with the committee on ordination. I was not looking forward to it. How would the committee respond to me?

I did well to be afraid. Sure enough, after a few niceties and a glance at my transcript (which was not stellar in those days) they got down to what I could tell was the issue of their real concern: Have you ever been in any relationship that one might consider to be gay? It seemed a roundabout way of asking the question. But the end result was (they thought) going to be clear;

this would weed out any undesirables. And I learned later they had already decided I was one of those anyway.

With great nervousness and anxiety I stammered something about how I didn't want to answer that question because I did not see that it had any relevance to ministry. (Damn. Why couldn't I remember any of the great answers we'd come up with when we'd practiced this a few weeks before?)

"We feel it *is* relevant," the chairperson said icily, "and so I'll ask it again."

"I can't answer," I said.

At that point, one of the other members of the committee saved the day – for them at least. "I think we all know that you are in fact gay and if you're not going to answer the question then you leave us no choice. I don't believe we can proceed with your request for ordination."

The chairperson said they would discuss things without me and let me know, but I could tell she was relieved with the way in which the other committee member had put things. They had taken care of what concerned them – I could be eliminated from the list of troublemakers who wanted to become a minister. I imagined them rubbing their hands and saying, "Phew, done and dusted," as soon as I left the room.

* * *

It didn't sink in at first, but I soon realized that I had just been told that The United Church of Canada would not ordain me, that I had no future in the denomination – the only church I had ever really known, other than a brief dabble in Anglicanism in my early teens.

No. Future. For. Me.

As the words formed in my brain, I realized the full import of it all. They didn't want me. They didn't want me because I was gay, because of who I was. Wow.

Given that I later went on to be ordained, and to serve several parishes in two U.S. denominations, and that the United Church offered me an apology when I came back 30-plus years later, I now can say, "more fool you."

But, at the time, I was gutted. How dare they? Bastards. What right did they have to make such a decision? It was a stupid question because they had, according to the rules of the United Church, every right. And they chose to exercise it.

I talked about this with friends. I got drunk. I talked about it some more. I had a terrible time trying to accept it.

A couple of my friends were very supportive and suggested that there were a number of things I could do to fight the decision, and that it was all going to turn out in the end. But I was not prepared to wait for the end – not by a long shot.

I was seeing Geoff at this time, and he told me about the possibility of a church in New York. I leapt at the chance.

It was in the U.S.? So what? You guys (that would be Canada, the United Church, whomever) don't want me? Good riddance – I'm packing my bags and heading south.

* * *

If one church was not going to recognize my call to ministry, then I would have to go elsewhere. I would knock on the door of a hundred denominations, I decided, if that's what it would take. Amazingly, I learned early on that if I behaved a little more modestly and kept my mouth shut, I didn't have too much difficulty. As it turned out, the United Methodist Church accepted me with open arms, licensing me as a local pastor almost immediately and then ordaining me a few years later.

* * *

When I moved to the U.S. and to the United Methodist Church, I had scurried back inside the closet. It was easy to do because I had no past in upstate New York and so to them I just seemed like your average eligible bachelor who was going to find the right woman and settle down. It was easy enough to pull off, although from the beginning some folks wondered about me. I've never been the most masculine of men. That said, blatant masculinity doesn't necessarily indicate anything and can sometimes even be used as a cover, especially considering the large number of truck drivers, prison guards, and other "tough men" who frequented the local rest area. I came to realize that gay and straight men come in all shapes and sizes and from every walk of life.

* * *

A lot of issues reared their heads in the 1980s and beyond in the United States. The Moral Majority was trying to impose a strict code on society while mistakenly calling it biblical; it wasn't, but many folks would decide what they wanted to believe and then go hunting for scripture verses to support it. They did this — and still do — in regards to a wide range of issues, such as abortion rights, homosexuality, marriage, and divorce (note how many of those are related to sexual matters) and also to things like nuclear disarmament and, at the time, sending arms to the government of El Salvador.

It seemed strange to me that someone like Oscar Romero could preach a gospel of peace, tolerance, land rights for the poor, and an end to government repression in El Salvador, and in North America we could be told that he was a communist and anti-Christian. When Romero was assassinated in 1980, many of us grieved terribly, but I know other church members who rejoiced.

When I first moved to the U.S., I was struck that so many

people thought there was a right way to do things, which could be supported by scripture, and a wrong way, which was clearly communist.

* * *

One of the things that always intrigued me was how we, as gay men, had to discover our gay heritage for ourselves. Obviously, it wasn't something our parents could share with us, since so many of them couldn't even acknowledge our homosexuality.

I suppose it's a little like the woman who was raised Roman Catholic and who, in her 70s, discovered that she was in fact Jewish – her biological parents had been killed in Auschwitz and a family adopted her, changing her identity to keep her alive. Suddenly, in her 70s, she found herself wanting (needing) to discover her real identity.

As gay men, we knew we were different and that there was a world of people and a culture attached to our identity, but it seemed somehow hidden. Our parents didn't share it, or couldn't, because of their own ignorance of it. Even for those who had a gay biological parent, it was apparently not something that was talked about.

I remember my parents sharing things about their past – which was by extension my own past. I knew of ancestors who were Scottish and Swedish, German and English. I knew of one grandfather who was born in Buenos Aires and of the other one who settled first in the U.S. and then came to Canada because he could get more farmland. But my gay heritage – that was a mystery, a "great unknown."

I had a friend who came out in his 30s. He had found a book in a thrift shop that told of 100 famous people who were gay or lesbian. The book was older, and so it didn't include people such as Elton John, Freddie Mercury, or Jodie Foster. But it told of

Gertrude Stein and Oscar Wilde, and as he read the book his eyes opened and his demeanor relaxed.

"I thought I was the only one," he said. "I thought I was all alone. But there have been people like me for centuries."

* * *

For want of a better word, we lived in a kind of ghetto — not literally, but in terms of being isolated simply by who we loved. We found ourselves sleeping around because, frankly, we could. If parents were going to disown us, then suddenly their mores and values didn't seem to matter.

And if we were told repeatedly that we could never have permanent relationships, or have real love, should it have been a surprise that many of us gave up looking for it, hoping instead that a fling with this boy tonight, that boy tomorrow, would make up for the fact that we really wanted, at the end of it all, someone to come home to. It's only human.

* * *

The stigma was one of the worst things.

Any hint of AIDS meant that you'd been having sex with men. Later, as people learned that there were other ways to catch it, the stigma softened, but not by much. For many men, the trauma was compounded by the fact that your first admission of having AIDS was also your first admission of being gay, or at least of having had the occasional gay fling; it amazed me the men who desperately tried to hang on to what they thought was a tiny shred of dignity by telling the world they were bisexual, or that they had been "experimenting." The truth was, in the first days, everyone knew you got AIDS from sex with other gay men, and generally from anal sex. So there was the additional stigma of admitting you liked that sort of thing. Society was still coming to grips with admitting that sex – of any kind – was okay, and that a person could enjoy it with no strings attached, so gay sex was a step too far.

* * *

There were a lot of misconceptions in the early days, including the idea that it was all a big hoax. Someone – big pharma, right-wing Christians, conservatives, Republicans in the U.S., take your pick – had created this scare to try to get gays to change their ways.

The response of the gay community was pretty predictable. For too long people had told us who we were allowed to have sex with (or more precisely, who we could *not* have sex with) and there was no way we were going to listen to that crap anymore. You couldn't tell me who to sleep with. Leave me alone. Go live your life, and I'll live mine.

That was an attitude that, sadly, killed a lot of men.

* * *

There was also the Patient Zero theory. This one came to great light in Randy Shilts' book *And the Band Played On* and made its way repeatedly around conversations in gay bars and coffee shops all over Montreal.

Shilts put forward the idea that one person (whom he called Patient Zero) was responsible for starting the spread of AIDS. The virus seemed to have originated somewhere in central Africa. It was at least surmised that an animal (maybe a chimp or gorilla caught in a trap) had passed the disease to a human, possibly through a bite. This person then had sex with several prostitutes and, depending on the story you heard, had sex with several men.

It so happened, the story went, that a flight attendant from Quebec, Gaëtan Dugas, slept with someone in Zambia — occasionally the story said it was Zimbabwe, or South Africa — and contracted AIDS. Being a flight attendant and having a voracious sexual appetite, Dugas slept with different men in different cities around the world each time he had a layover, and that's how AIDS spread.

It didn't help that Dugas himself did in fact claim to have slept with over 2,500 men since the early 1970s, and kept at it until his death from AIDS complications in 1984. And there was evidence that several early cases in New York and San Francisco were found in men who had slept with him. Or who had slept with someone else who had slept with him. Or who had slept with someone else who had slept with someone …

When Shilts published his book in 1987, it sold rapidly. People were fascinated with the Patient Zero theory. How convenient, to have one person to blame for it all. And when that person was gay, and a flight attendant, and a French-Canadian — well, it made it all just that much easier to believe.

I remember my friend Rob eagerly trying to debunk the Patient Zero theory. Rob had lived his entire life in Quebec and although he was anglophone he spoke French better than the rest of us and felt a deep affinity to the French-speaking community. He also had a francophone boyfriend, and that may have played into it.

"It's just too easy," he would say. "It's too easy to blame one person. And don't you think it's a bit suspicious that he's a French-speaking Quebecois? I mean, in Canada it's just too easy to blame someone who's French for almost anything."

Others would counter that he was just biased, that the theory made sense. People could even draw charts showing how the disease could spread exponentially, all from one source. Why wouldn't it be Dugas? After all, so-and-so slept with him.

That was the odd rub for us in Montreal. There were people we knew who actually *knew* Gaëtan Dugas, and had even slept with him, or knew someone who had. Or at least said they knew someone who knew someone who had. That's how things went in our community. Long before urban myths could circulate and replicate like wildfire on social media there was the gay network, conversations slightly below the surface that were bitchy and cutting and, at times, downright brutal. Many decades on, when scientists had debunked the Patient Zero theory — and even if Gaëtan Dugas had slept with hundreds of men after he himself became infected — it didn't matter. Times, thoughts, and realities had moved on. Even the publisher of Shilts' book later admitted he pushed the Patient Zero theory because he knew it would sell books, and he came to regret it.

* * *

My purple rash went away, but it took its own sweet time. It had begun only in the middle of my abdomen and slowly, over a period of several days, spread to my arms and legs. As it did so, my abdomen began to clear up, to the point that one day I had purple shins and forearms, but everything else looked normal. As I looked at myself naked in the mirror, I thought, "This is a warning. Most people don't get this. This is a warning that I've been spared this time. I will not be so lucky next time, I know it. Only safe sex from now on. And no more taking life for granted. It's too precious."

* * *

Geoff was a whirlwind romance that turned into an amazing friendship. It was more of a romance on my part than on his, I later discovered, but it was wonderful when it happened.

It was the relationship with Geoff that took me to the United States. That's where he lived, and he often spoke about how easy it was to get a church to serve in the northern part of New York state, because for most Americans it seemed like the end of the world (no matter that there was a whole other country a few miles north).

When the United Church of Canada decreed in 1982 that that they would not ordain me, I decided I would try for a church in New York and discovered it was quite easy; I just had to smile and say the right things to the District Superintendent (someone we called a "mini-bishop"), who had the authority to appoint people to serve small, usually rural churches. In short order, I got appointed to serve three small United Methodist congregations in upstate New York, just south of Montreal.

It helped immensely, of course, that I neglected to tell anyone in the United Methodist Church that I was gay.

* * *

Part of me missed the United Church of Canada, and missed living in Canada, period. I felt somewhat as though I were in exile. Friends in Canada could not for the life of them understand why I would move to the U.S. in the first place. This was the era of Ronald Reagan for heaven's sake – what was I thinking? Was any love affair really worth *that?*

One friend got especially angry when he realized I had gone back into the closet. I tried to explain that I needed to do that in order to get ordained in the church, and to serve the church, which is what I felt called to do. He said I was just being chicken.

Truth be told, I probably was. I wasn't about to waste several years of university study just to make a stand. No, if I had to be in the closet in order to do what I thought I should do, then I would. Surely it couldn't be that bad.

***

I became a regular at the local gay bar. There weren't many other places where gays could freely gather in the 1980s. I quickly earned the nickname "Reverend," which was spoken with a wide variety of nuances depending on the circumstances. Because it was such a huge Roman Catholic area, most people couldn't really understand how I was a priest (their word, never mine) and yet was down-to-earth. I took that as a compliment, even when it wasn't intended that way.

***

For the first couple years I lived in the U.S., I continued to commute to Montreal for school. This gave me the outlet of living in one community and being a minister, while I could still go to the big and wild city and be unabashedly gay – especially when people from that part of upstate New York almost never ventured north of the border. Some people might see that as difficult, to live in two worlds, but I found it simple. It was much easier to shut off one world at the border, in either direction, and embrace the other world. Switching back and forth was not difficult, and it kept me sane.

***

In the mid-1980s, I got married. It was a dumb idea.

I cannot say it was a loveless marriage – it was full of love. And it was at times happy. But it was a dumb idea. For a gay man to marry a straight woman is seldom a good idea. I know of a few couples who have gone into this with their eyes wide open, and others who have discovered things about each other (sometimes in less than pleasant ways) as time went on. But even when you know what you're doing, it's not a good idea. Someone almost always gets hurt.

I had been dating Margaret for about a month when I told her I was gay. I remember her first question: "Were you just experimenting?"

"No," I said. "I'm gay. And at the same time, I love you." I meant it. I really did. I'm not sure what else was going on, but I know it was real. It was also dumb. I know, I'm repeating myself, but it's because I should have admitted it then. The day before the wedding I remember thinking, "Oh God, what am I doing? Is it too late to get out of this?" But I went through with it.

We were married for 18 years, and some of those were good. Some of those were terrible. I didn't often want to admit it, but I knew that I desperately, constantly, craved being with a man. I just wasn't the right fit for a straight marriage, and I never would be.

* * *

Margaret and I became foster parents, and through that ended up adopting three children. They have become wonderful adults. If nothing else ever came out of the marriage, the fact that we raised three kids and they in turn have families of their own and are living good lives counts for something, I believe. But it wasn't right.

* * *

The biggest frustration in the marriage – even though I seldom admitted it to myself – was that I simply wanted to be rid of it. I wanted to be with a man. I belonged with a man.

However, as I said, I had trouble admitting this much of the time. I thought if I just tried harder, I could pull it off. It didn't work, although on the outside it appeared to; people saw us as the model family: me the young minister, Margaret the proper minister's wife, and our three children – the very picture of normal. Except it wasn't normal. It was a dystopian reality in which I tried to fit each day and was miserable to the core because of it all.

* * *

We moved. A lot.

I realize now that I was trying to run away, although at the time I didn't realize that I was trying to run away from the straight lifestyle. We moved to Vermont, then Hawaii, then Minnesota. It was in Minnesota that I reached the deepest parts of my depression.

I was often in a near catatonic state, simply staring straight ahead, not moving, and not even aware of where I was looking. It was horrible, and just frightening enough that I knew I needed professional help. I was referred to a psychiatrist at an agency run by the Roman Catholic Church. As it turns out, it was housed in a community centre in a predominantly black neighbourhood in Minneapolis.

I phoned to make an appointment and got the doctor's answering service. He had a nice, calm voice, and I imagined he was a kind young man, clearly established in a wholesome, straight marriage, and would provide me with just the right words of wisdom to help me get back on track and make my attempt at a straight lifestyle work.

I got an appointment, and I went in. I had so much hope. This was going to help me. And it did – although not in the ways I had expected.

We talked. The doctor wanted to know, of course, what had brought me to this moment, what had inspired me to come in and see him. As I told my story – in somewhat abbreviated form

– he smiled gently. When I stopped for breath, he looked straight at me.

"You've been trying to run away from something, and that's why you keep moving. The thing is, there's still one thing you have to break away from, and you haven't done it."

I looked a bit puzzled, but I didn't say anything.

"You need to leave your marriage. You don't fit. You'll never fit, because you're a gay man in a straight marriage. It doesn't work. It will never work."

I was shocked, yet at the same time I felt such a massive weight lift off me. He was right. I knew he was right. Deep down, I had probably known for years he was right, long before I heard a word from his mouth or even met him. Because hadn't I known it from the beginning? Hadn't I known that this would never work? Round peg, square hole – of course it wouldn't work. It was no one's fault, it was just reality.

* * *

I told Margaret that I needed to get out because I was a gay man.

"No, you're not," she told me, and cried tears of confusion, anger, and frustration – the last because I think deep down she knew this was real, she just didn't want it to be.

"But I am – you know that. I told you that."

"Yeah, but I assumed that because you were married to me for 18 years that you had outgrown that, that it was behind you."

I wanted to be angry. I wanted to say something crass like, "How could you be so stupid? Why would you think I would change?" Except, of course, she made a fair point. We had, after all, been together as a married couple, faithful to each other for 18 years. Why *wouldn't* she think things had changed?

But I knew that they hadn't, and that they couldn't. I needed to cut her some slack. I didn't at the time, but over the years it's become easier, and I've come to realize some of the position she was in. I had been going through my own struggles and anxiety-ridden nightmares, but she was quite oblivious to all this, and my statement did indeed take her by surprise.

* * *

I've often been asked why I got married in the first place. The most truthful and honest answer is that I don't really know. I mean, there were a lot of reasons — and many of them came into play. Margaret was not just my "beard" to use the expression often thrust upon a woman who stands by the side of a gay man to make him look more butch and thus more "normal."

I did love her, and I craved the "normalcy" that being married could give. I also think that, subconsciously at least, I needed something that would take me out of the lifestyle where I stood a good chance of catching AIDS. My illness in late 1983 scared the piss out of me, and I did not know any rational way to get out of it.

One day, prior to a church supper, I overheard someone in my church say to another person, "You should come to the dinner tomorrow and see the woman I've fixed the minister up with."

I thought, "This could be my chance. Marry a woman ... surely if I'm actually *married* to a woman I'll enjoy sex with her. And I won't need a relationship with a man because, well, I won't need the sex if I'm having sex with her."

I know now that who I was in a relationship with was about far more than just sex, and that that was a major part of the "problem" in the marriage, but at the time I was naïve enough to believe the myth that being gay was simply about who you had sex with. Or at least I wanted to believe it.

It was a blind date, and yet I pursued her. I wanted to get the transaction — which is mostly what it was — taken care of. It was, I discovered, much easier than I had imagined. Despite the rumours that had fluttered around, the reality was that no one wanted to believe anyone was *really* gay, and so if you did anything that fit within the "normal" range (and dating a woman surely qualified), then you were safe.

We dated for a little while, and we got married. And I'll say it once more. It was a dumb idea.

* * *

Geoff did the ceremony. That may seem strange, but to me and to him it seemed the way to do it. We were the best of friends, even if we were no longer lovers.

* * *

Margaret and I divorced in 2000. It was not pretty. In fact, it was messy and horrible and painful, maybe more so for her than for me. We had 18 years' worth of feelings and misunderstandings to untangle. And we had two teenage daughters at home to deal with, although I think they handled the divorce better than either Margaret or I did at times.

Then, in the midst of all this, our elder daughter informed us she was pregnant, at 16 years old. This caused a major "lump in the throat" moment for both Margaret and me. Still, in my mind, it couldn't change anything else. We still needed to separate. The anger and animosity that had been building up in me for almost two decades needed to be released or something bad would happen, although I had no idea what.

I moved first into the basement, and then right around the time our granddaughter arrived I moved into an apartment about halfway between the house and my place of work, which was good as we were sharing one car. The timing wasn't great, but it wasn't the end of the world, either. In fact, nothing in this whole thing was the end of the world; I was convinced of that, even if Margaret wasn't. She had imagined a lifetime together and it had been ripped away from her. From where I was standing it was inevitable; from where she was standing it was horrible.

I received a lot of support from the church. Although I was not serving a congregation at the time, I *was* still working with the church in that I was working for a publishing company that created and distributed church resources.

Because I wasn't serving a congregation, I had the luxury of attending a variety of churches, and I took advantage of this to visit Spirit of the Lakes United Church of Christ. They were a relatively new church that worshipped in a former supermarket in Minneapolis. While open to everyone, they especially catered to the LGBTQ+ community.

I was struck by a number of things the Sunday I attended. One was that I was warmly welcomed when I first went in and was invited to sit wherever I wanted, However, the person who greeted me invited me, if I'd like, to sit with him and his partner. I appreciated the gracious invitation that was presented in such a way I knew I could say "no" and no offence would be taken.

I said yes, and he took me to a seat beside someone in a wheelchair, promptly introducing me to the fellow in the wheelchair as his partner. I sat down, and he told me a little about the church, including that they had communion every Sunday. Everyone was welcome to participate in communion, and people would go up to the front in small groups to receive the elements. Afterwards, those who wished could meet with others at the front who would pray with them for any concerns they had.

I was never big on requesting prayers, but after communion I joined a small cluster of people who welcomed me with loving smiles and asked if I had concerns to share. I said something like, "My marriage and home are breaking up and it's painful even though it's the right thing to do." They nodded knowingly and prayed with me. It felt good. There was no judgment, no commentary, just a willingness to offer a concern to the Divine and know that it was heard.

After the service I recognized someone – the only person there that I knew. She was a transgender woman I had heard speak at an event one time, and I went over to introduce myself. We chatted for a while and in the course of conversation over coffee I realized that she had been married (to a woman) before her transition. I asked her what it was like, ending her marriage when she did.

"It was hell. It's always hell to end something like that. But sometimes it's the thing you have to do. There are lots of things in life that we have to get through, even when they hurt. The thing to do is get through them while leaving as few bodies on the field as possible."

I thought it was a great image, and a helpful one for me. I would continue the painful process of ending my marriage while leaving as few bodies on the field as possible.

* * *

If anything, I had drifted away from God when I started in parish ministry. I found myself in the horrid and uncomfortable position of knowing I had to defend a strange set of beliefs, or at least acknowledge that people had a right to hold them, even when I knew they were blatantly wrong.

Years later I was on a list serve – a kind of a primitive forerunner to Facebook where, if you belonged to the group, you could send out messages that could be read by everyone in the group. This group was confined to United Methodist ministers in the region where I lived. One of ministers was, to put it politely, fanatically right wing – fiercely anti-gay, not afraid to tell someone to their face that they were going to hell for any number of reasons, and always convinced he was right. Period.

He didn't like me very much (not really a surprise). He and I would frequently spar on the list serve and drag others into our arguments. Years later, after I had already retired from the United Methodist Church and moved to the United Church of Christ, he decided to take things further. He sought support from others in an attempt to deny me access to my United Methodist pension when I turned 62 – because I was gay. (I was "out" by this time.) Thankfully, he didn't get much support. Still, it was not a pleasant argument to carry out in front of others. I tried to get away from it, but it was hard to do because he kept saying things about me on the list serve, and I couldn't help but respond.

What was affirming is that most of my colleagues would not agree with him, no matter (or perhaps because of) how hard he whined and complained and ranted about how I was destroying the world as we knew it.

Just prior to the meeting where my retirement was to take effect, he said he was going to stand up and demand that my ministry be struck – obviously it had not been real ministry because of who I was.

I thought about it and came up with an answer to him. I said, "Will you contact all the people I married and tell them they are not married, because my ministry was invalid? Will you contact the people I baptized and tell them that they have no place in the church because, unbeknownst to them, their baptism doesn't count because I did it? And would he also contact those who felt touched or moved by something I might have said in a sermon, to tell them they were mistaken?"

How do you nullify something someone has done, because of who they are? Even when the church strips someone of their ordination, it does not typically claim that the person's ministry didn't take place.

The effect of all of this was positive and affirming to me, because through his silly ranting and raving I had to address some of my thoughts and misgivings, and the experience strengthened my faith. I hadn't done anything wrong and my ministry "counted," no matter what this person thought. It takes more than one person's ideas — even more than a committee's ideas — to render something "unworthy" when most others think it is important and worthy.

* * *

I had a similar experience in the 2000s at an *'Aha o na Kahu* meeting. This was a gathering of the *kahu* (ministers) serving churches in the United Church of Christ that were Hawaiian in language and heritage. I was serving such a church in Lahaina on the island of Maui at the time.

But let me back up. When I first moved to Hawaii, I left full-time parish ministry for a while. I had been working part-time on a Sunday school curriculum project for several years and it turned into a full-time job if I wanted it. I struggled with whether or not to take the leap but decided to do it. I loved working as a writer and an editor, and this was an exciting resource.

While that was my major employment, I *did* serve a small Hawaiian church on a very part-time basis. This was a powerful learning experience. People often do not realize that Hawaiian culture, prior to the arrival of New England missionaries in 1820, was quite open and tolerant. It recognized differences amongst people and, for the most part, made allowances for such differences and personalities within society. Then along came the missionaries who thought this was terribly wrong — you needed to believe the way they did, or else. It was that simple.

One Hawaiian congregation forbid hula in worship because they were convinced that dancing was a disgrace and mortal sin.

I tried to dissuade them and talked about how hula could be used as a wonderful way to interpret hymns, etc., but they would hear none of it. Dancing was evil. Moving your body in any way in response to music was evil. That particular congregation discouraged people from even swaying while singing hymns.

To this day, the Hawaiian church consists of this odd mix of people wanting to be tolerant and accepting but hearing loud missionary voices telling them that they'd better watch it or they'll all burn in hell.

So ... I'm at the semi-annual *'Aha o na Kahu* on the Big Island and by this point it's pretty well known that I'm gay. That put me in a minority of one amongst a group of about 40. Several of the 40 were pretty tolerant and got along with me fine. But there were some who were vehemently opposed to, and challenged by, my presence, if not my existence. How could I claim any right to serve a Hawaiian church – or frankly any Christian church – while living such a frightening and repugnant lifestyle?

It was a hot evening and we had been doing a lot of business, and then one of the other *kahu* stood up. (Hawaiian clergy always simply refer to other clergy as *kahu*.) "I know that some are troubled by burdens they carry." He looked directly at me. "Some of us don't even know the burdens we carry. Satan gets in there and convinces us that we're all right when all the while we're going to hell, and we're taking our congregations to hell. But there's help. We can heal you." Again, he stared straight at me. "We can. I've been to West Hollywood; I know what it's like. I know what you're going through. But right here, right now, we can heal you."

He went on, and a few people began to squirm in their seats. Sitting right in front of me was another right-wing *kahu* and I expected him to support this guy who was speaking. I'll never forget it. Kalani (the one in front of me) turned and said, "I'm sorry."

"Huh?" I asked, kind of stupefied by the whole thing.

"I'm sorry – I don't agree with what he's saying." He quickly added, "I don't agree with you and what you're doing, either. But that's your business. You don't have to sit through this." At Kalani's urging, I got up and left.

The lesson for me was two-fold: first, there are strange people in the world who have strange ideas, and sometimes they'll try to impose their strange ideas on you; second, you don't have to take it.

***

I learned a great deal from Hawaiians about how to deal with differences in the world. I was living on Maui when I got married to George (in Canada). When we returned to Maui, we decided that we should not hide our relationship, but be honest and up front about it. It was the rockiest of roads, but I think we came through it all okay.

As I went around to tell people in the congregation, I knew I had to tell a very significant couple who held a great deal of sway. He was Hawaiian and she was Japanese. I phoned and told them I needed to come over and talk to them. Then off I went to see Aunty and Uncle (that's what you call Hawaiians who you respect) – in fear and trembling.

I sat down, took a deep breath, and said, "Aunty, Uncle, I wanted you to know that I'm in a relationship with a man."

"I know," Aunty said, to let me know that I couldn't pull anything over on *her*.

"And do I understand," she continued, "that you've married this man? Why?"

"Well," I said, sweating profusely, "we love each other, and I wouldn't live in the *hale kahu* (the manse) with a woman I wasn't married to."

"Can you get an annulment?" The question threw me.

"Why would I do that?" I stammered.

"Because *I* don't like it."

At this point Uncle joined the conversation. "I'm not *ma'a* with this." *Ma'a* is a Hawaiian word roughly meaning "comfortable" or "familiar."

We chatted a bit more. I was so nervous things just bounced around in my head and I cannot for the life of me remember how the rest of the visit went, but after a time I left. I was scared, because I knew that if they did not like a situation they could take care of it. Taking care of it, in that culture, meant making the thing go away. And in this situation the "thing" was me and my husband. I was scared.

A few weeks later there was some conversation about all this after church. Several people shared their opinions (some positive, some negative), and then Aunty stood up.

"I think you know Daddy (that's what she called Uncle) and I have had some trouble with all this. We've talked about it for a long time, and we've prayed about it. I didn't like it. I didn't like it at all. But I thought about it some more. We like *Kahu*. And over the past little while we've gotten to know George, too. I like *Kahu's* sermons, and his Bible class, and the way he takes care of the church. So I'm fine with this now."

She sat down, but there was no doubt in the room as to what her final short sentence had really meant: "I'm fine with this, so you'd all better be, too. This situation is now over."

I know they were never really comfortable with my marriage to George, nor even with the fact that I was gay, but they came to realize that maybe that wasn't their business.

* * *

My church in Hawaii served lunch every Sunday after worship. We also attracted a lot of tourists as our town was a destination for holidaying folks from North America, and many of them loved to attend a Hawaiian church where they could sing Hawaiian hymns and be exposed to a familiar brand of Christianity but in different cultural packaging.

I would often sit with visitors during lunch. On one particular Sunday we had a couple visiting us from the state of Georgia, and I sat with them along with the moderator of the church and a couple others. George was sitting at another table nearby.

"Pastor," the Georgian visitor said in that particular drawl unique to southerners, "you haven't introduced us to your better half. You've got to have a pretty little wife around here somewhere."

I paused slightly. I caught the eye of the moderator who, without uttering a word, seemed to say, "Let's deflect this one and not open a can of worms." I pretended I didn't hear him, and went on with some other part of the conversation. A few moments later, though, he raised the issue again, this time with more insistence.

"When are you going to introduce us to your pretty little wife?" He looked around. "You've got to have a pretty little wife around here somewhere."

At that point, George leaned over from his table and said calmly and serenely, "That would be me." He held up his left hand and displayed his wedding ring.

The couple from Georgia got up and departed so quickly I'd swear they left skid marks on the church parking lot.

* * *

Another experience involved Uncle Bob, a Hawaiian *kahu* from the Big Island. I was teaching a class on the Big Island for people preparing for lay ministry, and several folks from Uncle Bob's church attended. One of them did not like me — I was too liberal for his radically conservative theology — and thought he had a great opportunity to get rid of me by going to Uncle Bob and complaining that I was gay. He was convinced that I would be fired within minutes. Boy was he wrong.

Uncle Bob told me about this some time later. "I got mad at him, I tell you. I got so mad at him. I said, 'You cannot condemn this *kahu*, just because you don't like him. He is a *kahu* of the church, and it's not our place to judge.' But I don't mind telling you, *Kahu* (and he was speaking to me from his heart at this point), I struggle with all this. I don't believe I have ever known anyone like you (gay), let alone a *kahu* who is like you. But in my culture, that's my problem. I have to find a way to accept you. We don't believe that you have to change; we believe we have to find a way to understand and accept you."

Several months later I saw Uncle Bob at a meeting. He walked over to me and simply said, "I'm fine with everything now." And he gave me a hug. We never discussed it again.

Several years after that, when Uncle Bob had been dead for some time, I was talking with his son. "My father had great respect for you," he told me. "He said you taught him a great deal about loving your neighbour."

That was probably one of the greatest compliments anyone has ever given me.

***

I met George when I was living on Maui. Like me, he had moved there from the U.S. mainland. He was a recovering alcoholic, and I knew from the start he had trouble with the recovery part. When he lapsed from recovery, he could drink in ways that defied comprehension. I once took him to the hospital when he had gotten horribly drunk, and they did a breathalyzer on him. He registered .36 blood alcohol content, yet he was able to walk and his language was lucid. To put things in perspective, any reading above .3 is considered life-threatening. He was .06 over that and functioning relatively well.

Despite all this, I fell for him. I was the minister of the local Hawaiian church and he was a two-bit homeless drunk, but it didn't seem to matter.

After a few months together, we travelled to Canada. I had to attend a meeting there, and we arranged that he would meet me at the end of it and then we'd go visit my parents. Shortly before our trip we had decided to get married, because gay marriage had just been legalized in Canada. We had spoken to the minister at my parents' church and he had agreed to do the ceremony. I had also spoken with a friend of mine and he said we could get married in his yard. The thing was, my parents were away on vacation just before we arrived, so I had not had a chance to share any of this information with them.

We were sitting around with my parents and my mother asked nonchalantly, "So, do you have any plans for your time here?" We both burst out laughing.

"What's so funny?" she wanted to know.

Deep breath. "Well, one thing we're planning on doing is getting married."

"Oh," she said.

"I see," my father said.

We chatted while things sank in for them. What was wonderful is that there was nothing in their reaction to suggest anything other than the fullest love and support. Then my father got drawn away by a phone call.

"Doug's willing to perform the marriage, and we're going to get married at Nick's place."

"Well, I think that sounds wonderful," my mother said.

Dad got off the phone and came back to the living room. "I think that's great, if that's what you want to do," he said, and after a moment, "Hey, the mill picnic is this week. If you guys aren't doing anything I'd love to take you and introduce you to some of the guys from work."

George and I quickly declined, although we thanked him profusely. Somehow, being introduced as "my gay son and the man he's about to marry" to a bunch of millworkers who had had a few beers didn't sound like the most fun, or safe, environment to find ourselves in. But George and I would often say afterwards how incredibly loving a gesture it was — that my father, who had struggled so much with me when I was a teenager, had now gone beyond mere tolerance and had arrived at this wonderful place of love and acceptance. I had always known my parents were capable of this, that it was a value they had instilled in me. Now I saw it in action.

* * *

We went to my friend's house early on the day of the wedding and swam in the river. It was one of the coldest damn rivers I had ever been in in my life, but there was something quite wonderful about doing something like this in the midst of everything else — it kind of kept things in perspective.

After the ceremony, a small handful of us went out for dinner. My parents paid. "It's appropriate to pay for the reception," my mother said.

What I didn't know was that a day or two later she sent information about the wedding to the local paper, and in due course they printed our picture and a brief wedding notice. Given that neither of us wore a white dress most people could probably deduce it was a gay wedding. The day after it appeared someone phoned my mother and thanked her for doing that. "I wish I had had the same courage," the woman said, "when my son and his partner got married."

* * *

One of the strangest – and most difficult – things about getting married in Canada and returning to the U.S. at that time was that we were so thrilled to be married. Yet as we went to cross the border we realized that we were *not* married in the U.S., and given that we were of the same gender with different last names (thus, not related in American legal eyes) we had to fill out separate customs and immigration forms. It was a small thing, but it stung. Most newlyweds going home wouldn't have to face this, and it stung.

* * *

A few people at my church were upset with my situation. Interestingly, these were all people who were not active in the congregation and who seldom attended. But they considered themselves to be a part of the church and they decided to raise a bit of a stink.

"You should have told us you were gay when we interviewed you," one of them said. "You lied to us."

"I didn't lie," I said. "The issue never came up."

"Yeah, but because it never came up we all assumed you were straight."

A fellow on the board of deacons spoke up. "Excuse me, Aunty," he said. "I didn't."

Everyone wanted to ignore him and continued their conversation.

"Excuse me," he said a little louder. "I didn't think *Kahu* was straight. I could tell he was gay. But I didn't think it had anything to do with whether he'd make a good *kahu* or not."

It was a simple statement, but it spoke volumes.

* * *

In the midst of this, George and I got our 15 minutes of fame. Someone – I'll never know who – sent our story to *The Advocate* magazine, a national gay monthly. They were doing a feature on "the top 75 coming out stories of the year" and lo and behold they decided they wanted to include us.

Not only that, they wanted to feature us on the cover.

Wow.

Double wow.

Triple and quadruple and quintuple wow.

This was big.

George and I talked about it and agreed that if a magazine like this wanted to publicize our story, we should let them. So we wrote up the story and sent it in with a picture. Sure enough, the magazine said the picture was great and they would feature us on the cover. We held our breath.

Then hurricane Katrina hit the U.S. mainland, and our picture was confined to a postage-stamp-size image in the corner, as the hurricane took centre stage. Just for good measure I drove across the island to the one bookstore and bought all four copies they had.

Was I nervous about people reacting?

Yeah. Maui could be a very small island sometimes.

* * *

A conversation I had with Uncle Laki helped put some things in perspective.

Uncle Laki never came to church. He was nominally a member of the congregation, but no one could ever remember seeing him at worship. His wife was Roman Catholic, but he didn't accompany her there, either. None of this stopped him from coming to register his opinion with me, though.

He made an appointment to see me and we sat outside on a bench at the church. "I'll tell you why I don't come to church, *kahu*," he said.

"This ought to be good," I thought to myself. He hasn't been here all his adult life — and now he wants to tell me why?

"I can't come to church, because I can't sit there in the pew looking at you and imagining you in bed with a man. That just turns my stomach, and it's all I can think about when I see you."

I decided to jump in with all four feet; I had nothing to lose.

"Tell me, Uncle, when the previous *kahu* was here did you look at her and imagine her in bed with her husband?"

Uncle Laki looked at me kind of funny, but he didn't say anything.

"I gotta say, Uncle, I find it kind of creepy that you look at me and imagine me having sex. Just for the record, whenever I look at *you* I do *not* imagine you and Aunty having sex. So why do you do that with me?"

He had clearly not expected the conversation to go like this. I don't know if he thought I would offer a grand apology and promise never to have sex with a man ever again, but I couldn't let it go. I had had it.

"Uncle," I said, standing up, "I think it's probably good you don't come to church. I would be really uncomfortable trying to preach knowing that someone in the congregation was imagining me having sex. I find that kind of creepy." I paused. "I find that *really* creepy."

I walked away and went in the church office. When I came out several moments later to go home, he was nowhere around.

Granted, I was hardly pastoral in my response to him. In fact, I was downright rude. But his statement brought to a boil something that had been brewing inside me for a long time.

Why did people want to think about me having sex? I have run into people who seem to be obsessed with my sex life, and that disturbs me. I am *not* my sex life any more than another person is theirs. I am much, much more than that. We all are.

When you reduce me, or any other person regardless of their sexuality, to someone who has sex in a certain way, you insult me terribly. You want to define me solely by what I do with my genitalia.

Yeah, that's creepy.

* * *

I had a good friend in Hawaii – a fellow minister – who was also gay. We had long talks about what it was like to be gay and Christian. He was, by birth, a Hawaiian and had lived all his life there. The voices of missionaries still ring very loudly in the ears of many Hawaiian people, and they approach their faith with a good dose of fear.

"I envy you, Kahu," he said to me. "You live with your partner in the *hale kahu* and you're open about your sexuality. I've never been able to do that."

"Why do you think that is?" I asked him gently.

"I'm scared. I don't think it's wrong – I really don't – but just in case it is, I don't want to risk eternity just for some enjoyment now."

I wasn't sure I was understanding correctly, so I pressed a little.

"What do you mean by 'risking eternity'? I don't quite understand."

He hesitated, not wanting to offend me. "I really don't think it's wrong," he repeated. "But maybe it is. Maybe God is doing this as a test. If I were to fail that test, and give in to my flesh, I could be damned forever."

I breathed. Deeply.

"Kahu, do you believe God loves you?" I asked.

"Of course I do!"

"Do you really think a loving God would condemn someone's soul to rot or burn for all eternity because of something they did in this lifetime – something that didn't hurt another person? Do you think that God would punish someone for simply loving someone else? Does that sound like a loving God to you?"

"No," he conceded, "it doesn't. But how can I be sure?"

We left it at that, and I always feel a sadness for him whenever I think of this conversation. He had denied himself the possibility of a loving relationship, and companionship, because he feared that God would destroy him eternally.

It makes no sense to me, and it sickens me to think that Christians have for centuries tried to spew such filth on the LGBTQ+ community. It's wrong. Just plain wrong.

*　*　*

When I left Hawaii and moved back to the U.S. mainland, I served two churches in the Seattle area. In both cases I went to the church as an out gay man, with my partner in tow, and no one seemed to bat an eye. That was a breath of fresh air, especially after some of the hostility I had experienced in Hawaii and prior to that in the United Methodist Church. In fact, I came to realize that a large percentage of the clergy in the Seattle area seemed to be gay or lesbian. Maybe it had something to do with the progressive nature of the Pacific Northwest. Or maybe they had just decided that it didn't matter.

I remember one time marching in the Pride parade in Seattle. Pride was pretty big in Seattle — they even flew a massive rainbow flag from the top of the Space Needle — and it was a pretty cool experience

There were a lot of folks from my church in the parade, and that was exciting and affirming. They suggested I wear a clerical collar (I had one, but almost never wore it) because they thought it was important for folks to see an obvious clergy person walking in the parade. I agreed to do it on one condition — I could hold hands with my (then) husband at the same time. They all thought that was pretty cool.

A lot of people noticed us and cheered for us, and even took our picture. However, I don't know if that was because of my collar, or because George was wearing a T-shirt that said, "Jesus had two daddies."

When I left the second church in Seattle to go back to Hawaii one last time, the congregation laughingly said that I could leave, but that George had to stay, because they had taken a particular shining to him. It felt good to have the congregation affirm that my partner was a part of the picture, and that he (and by extension I) belonged.

* * *

Back when I was living in Hawaii the first time, the government held a referendum on same-sex marriage. The referendum was precipitated by a lawsuit brought by a gay couple who had sought a marriage licence and were denied it on the basis of sex. The courts ruled in the couple's favour, but immediately suspended their ruling for six months and invited the government to try to resolve the issue.

There was vigorous debate on both sides, and the result of the referendum was that same sex-marriage would remain illegal in Hawaii for the time being. However, legal changes *did* come – changes that allowed same sex couples to share health insurance (a key issue in Hawaii), to have automatic inheritance rights if their partner died without a will, and, for some people most importantly, the right to visit a same-sex partner in hospital. Prior to this, that simple right had been denied.

That may not seem like much, but several years later when my partner and I entered into what was known as a "civil partnership" and he ended up in the hospital at one point, I was extremely grateful for the few pieces of equality that law had given us.

Several years later, when people realized that the world had *not* come to an end, and when no one could back up the argument that expanding the definition of marriage to include all couples would somehow weaken it, the Hawaiian legislature voted to allow same-sex marriage. Specifically, they removed the portion of the law that simply defined marriage as being between a man and a woman.

A couple days after the law was changed, a cartoon appeared in the local paper of a man standing at the altar of a church holding hands with a dog that was dressed as a bride. The minister was saying something like, "Boy, this stuff has sure gotten out of hand." It was a sentiment many people held, but it faded away pretty quickly.

* * *

One minister preached a sermon the Sunday after the law passed, railing on and on about how marriage was a sacred bond between a man and a woman and was designed for the sole purpose of producing children who would then be nurtured in a safe and appropriately heterosexual home. Except this minister and his wife had no children.

I said nothing to him about this until he chose to challenge me and my relationship with a man. While the issue of why he and his wife had no children was none of my business, I nonetheless found an appalling hypocrisy in the fact that he felt marriage was all about having children, and yet he and his wife had none.

"That's different," he said to me, angrily.

"How is it different?" I asked, as gently as I could.

"It just is."

We never spoke about that issue again.

* * *

My final stint in Hawaii was intriguing, as I was the first openly gay staff member of the Hawaii Conference United Church of Christ. This was a large denomination in Hawaii, the descendants of the first missionaries, and so my presence was not insignificant. A few people had decided that this was disgusting, to have a person of my ilk serving on the conference staff, but opposition soon faded. People came to accept that I was just another minister.

It was while I was in this job that my marriage to George ended in a way that was probably predictable yet also very painful. It took a lot out of me. What I had not expected, however, was that I would receive a sympathetic ear from not only fellow staff members, but also from people in several of the churches I served. This was new for me – and welcome. No one cared that the spouse who had tried to kill me and was now no longer a part of my life was a man, they just cared for me. I needed that affirmation and was so very grateful to receive it.

* * *

While I was in Hawaii, I was once asked to address the State Sunday School Association. (I'm quite certain that Hawaii is the only state with a Sunday School Association, it being a leftover from missionary days.) What surprised me about the invitation was the fact that it was from a pretty conservative organization, not noted for any kind of tolerance or acceptance of the LGBTQ+ community. I decided to raise this with the woman who invited me to speak.

"I'm intrigued you have thought of me," I said to her, "given that you folks have a stance of being opposed to gays and lesbians serving in ministry in the church."

"Of course we do," she answered very quickly.

"Then why do you want me to speak at your gathering? You know that I'm gay, right? And you know that I'm in a relationship with a man, right?"

She paused, but only for a moment. "Yes, but we like you." It seemed a strange answer, and could have been taken in a wide variety of ways.

"We don't think of you as being gay," she continued. "We just like you as a kahu."

I decided to speak to the group and as part of my address I talked about the need to be welcoming and accepting in our Sunday schools. I'm quite sure that while they all nodded in agreement it never dawned on them that such a welcome should be extended to LGBTQ+ folks. But at least I said it. And they *did* like me.

* * *

I left the Hawaii Conference after only two years; the reason I'll offer is "creative differences" over how things should be done. I also was tired. I had two failed marriages under my belt, I missed my children and grandchildren (all of whom lived on the U.S. mainland), and while I absolutely loved Hawaii, I was increasingly aware of how far away it was from the rest of civilization.

I explored moving to a number of places on the U.S. mainland, and then realized it was time to go back home to Canada. I missed a lot of things about Canada, not least of which was the atmosphere of tolerance that, while far from universal or perfect, was still miles ahead of anything in the United States. To be clear, I am well aware that Canada has been plagued by deep-rooted racism since its beginnings, and that there are still a lot of people in Canada who are far from tolerant of the LGBTQ+ community. But, overall, I knew it to be a more accepting place. I also knew that The United Church of Canada would be a good place to finish my career as a minister. So I quit my job, packed up all my books, and headed home.

* * *

I moved back to Canada at the end of 2015. Because of customs regulations, it was much less expensive to ship my things to the U.S. mainland than to Canada directly, so I did that and arranged with my dad to go to the U.S. to pick them up when they arrived.

I knew that this could be an adventure. I needed paperwork to identify the contents of each box and knew that Canada Customs could go through each and every box if they so desired. Armed with a sheaf of papers, I approached the desk and was greeted by the customs agent.

He took the papers, and asked me, "When did you move to the United States?"

"In 1982," I replied.

"And why are you moving back now?" he asked.

I knew I wasn't supposed to joke with the people at Customs and Immigration, but I was a little over-tired and so, without thinking of where I was, blurted out, "because Donald Trump might become president and I don't want to risk it."

Apparently, the agent agreed with me, or at least had a similar sense of humour, because he rubber-stamped my papers and sent us on our way.

* * *

Shortly before my return to Canada, the United Church of Christ in the U.S. and The United Church of Canada voted to mutually recognize each other's ministers. This meant that if you were a minister in one denomination you were considered a minister in the other denomination and could apply for churches in the other denomination without changing your standing.

This option was available to me as I sought a Canadian church, but I wanted standing in The United Church of Canada, specifically. While I had no regrets about the ministry I had been able to offer in the U.S. over many years, I wanted to finish my career as a United Church of Canada minister. So I applied for standing.

I was the first United Church of Christ minister to transfer to Canada since the new ruling, and so the Canadian church wasn't sure what to do with me at first. When I said I wanted standing, they arranged for me to meet with a committee at their semi-annual meeting, and so off I went to Vancouver.

I had not been living or working in Canada for most of my adult life and so I didn't expect to recognize anyone at the meeting. However, as I walked in the door, I bumped into a friend with whom I had worked for many years on curriculum development. He gave me a big hug and announced to the folks he was standing with "This man is one of the best ministers I've ever met" – or words to that effect. I was overwhelmed, but also pleased and relieved – that kind of endorsement surely could not hurt!

I was also aware that when I had been denied ordination in Montreal so many years previously, a note had been put in my file, so I was a bit hesitant. I knew that sexual orientation was no longer a roadblock to ministry in The United Church of Canada, but still, what on earth might they have put in my file 34 years ago? That I was insubordinate and mean-spirited and had fangs?

I met with the committee. To my pleasant surprise, someone I knew (who was also a former moderator of the United Church) was one of the people on the team of about six that was interviewing me. She began by saying, "Oh, I saw the name and I hoped it was you!" I figured that was another good sign.

The interviewing team talked to me about my ministry, and about what had brought me to this meeting. I told them about being denied ordination in 1982. They said it didn't matter, because the reason I was denied ordination was no longer relevant, the previous action was null and void. Seeing as there were no other blemishes on my career, they welcomed me into the United Church. I breathed a huge sigh of relief. I mean, that they would do so should not have been a surprise to me, but still I had been anxious. And I was not prepared for what happened next.

"We need to apologize to you," the chair of the team said.

"What? Oh, you don't need to do that," I said, feeling quite humbled just by the suggestion. "It's really okay. I've had a good run of ministry, and a lot of wonderful things have happened in my life that wouldn't have happened if things hadn't turned out the way they did, so no, you don't have to apologize to me."

"Yes, we do," he repeated, and the others nodded. "We need to apologize because what we did was wrong. We need to apologize as part of owning our behaviour."

They asked me to sit in the centre of the circle, and everyone laid hands on my head or shoulders. The chair then offered a sincere apology for the fact that the church had been blinded by factors that were not in keeping with the gospel, and because of that had denied me something I had deserved.

I was humbled.

Very humbled.

I did not think I needed this, and yet as the words were spoken and I absorbed them I found myself overwhelmed with gratitude. They had recognized that I had indeed been called by God to ministry, and that it was wrong of the church to have denied that. It was without question the most powerful moment I have ever experienced in the church.

I was home.

* * *

Today I am comfortable with where I have landed in my life and my ministry.

After my marriage to George ended, I figured that being part of a duo was no longer in the cards. However, I was blessed to meet Kevin on a blind date after I had been back in Canada for about a year.

I was nervous about the date, knowing that a lot of gay men fly out the door when they hear you have something to do with the church, so I played down my church work and emphasized my work in publishing, figuring that was slightly firmer ground.

"Oh," Kevin said. "My sister used to work for that same company." As it turned out, I had known – and worked with – Kevin's sister for about 30 years. When he texted her that evening to tell her who he had just had dinner with – and presumably to ask her if he ought to run for the hills – she told him *not* to run (thanks, Lois) and in fact wondered why she had never thought to introduce us before.

One of the great joys of finding a soulmate and companion at this stage of life is that you learn from life, you learn the mistakes not to make in a relationship, and, while I am far from perfect and still screw up from time to time, both Kevin and I are much easier people to live with.

* * *

Of course, there are still people who want to challenge my right to be in ministry, or to call myself Christian. To such people I want to ask (and I do if I get the opportunity), Is your God that small? Is your God that mean? Is your God that narrow-minded?

Do you really think that God says to me — or to anyone — that they are not good enough to be accepted as part of God's family, for *any* reason, let alone for their sexuality? Does God create us only to say to one-tenth of us, "Sorry, you don't make it"? Of course not.

The God I have encountered in scripture, the God who I have known all my life, the God I proudly serve does not do that to any of us. On the contrary, my God constantly affirms my place and calls me to acts of justice and kindness as part of my Christian living. Formal ministry is the way I chose to live out my vocation, but the truth is that God calls each of us who will dare to claim that we belong to God, and asks us to change the world, to make it a more loving and holy place. We are to take the gospel of hope and unconditional love into the cracks and corners of our world and tell those who have been hurt and rejected — especially those who have been hurt and rejected by the church — that they belong, and that *nothing* can change that. No one's angry words, hate-filled gestures, or name-calling can negate the work of God who made us, declared us to be good and invites us into a new and holy relationship with God, and with one another.

This God, whom I experience daily in the presence of the risen Christ in my life, is very much alive and very real for me.

This God is a companion and friend, one who invites me to be kind and compassionate to others, invites others to be the same, and who holds me accountable. I have no room for an angry, judgmental God – such a thing is merely an invention of those who wish to exert power over others.

Some acquaintances have taken great pains to let me know that they don't like me. They have been hurt by the church so badly that what I represent is abhorrent to them. Rather than dislike these people, I appreciate that they remind me of some of the horrific things that have been done in the name of God, things that were just plain wrong.

No one has the right to tell you that you are excluded, that you don't belong – no one.

The United Church of Christ used to make doormats that carried this phrase in the hopes that every congregation would put one at their front door: "No matter who you are or where you are on life's journey, you are welcome here."

When we are able to live that truth, the world becomes a better place.

A GLOSSARY

Please know that there are a variety of nuances to many of these words, and that they have other meanings, too. What I offer here is a quick explanation that should enable folks to have an intelligent discussion, and/or to understand things they are reading. You can Google them for more information, or find many of them discussed much more fully in other books and articles.

LGBTQQI2+ This is a common example of the alphabet soup that folks have come to use to describe "the community." It has grown and changed over the years, and you will undoubtedly find numerous other variations of it. The letters represent **L**esbian **G**ay **B**isexual **T**ransgendered **Q**ueer **Q**uestioning **I**ntersex **2**-spirit; the plus sign acts as a sort of an ellipsis, implying that there are others in this group. While it is a bit cumbersome, the truth it underscores is profound: there are vast numbers of people who find themselves at a variety of places on a spectrum between heterosexual and homosexual. The letters are a way of giving each a smidgin of representation within this broad community. **Note**: *I use the word "spectrum" below as an abbreviation for this term.*

Asexual A lack of sexual interest in, or attraction to, another person regardless of gender. Some see this as a legitimate sexual orientation while others see it as a lack of sexual orientation.

Binary The idea of something being in two parts. In the context of sexuality, this would be the archaic — and false — understanding that there are two genders, male and female, or two sexual orientations, gay or straight. Over time, especially in recent years, people are coming to embrace the reality that the eight billion plus people on this planet fit into more than just two categories.

Bisexual Someone who is sexually attracted to both men and women.

Cisgender A person whose gender identity matches the sex they were identified with at birth. For example, someone who sees themselves as a woman and who was born with a vagina would be cisgender. The opposite is *transgender* (see below).

Faggot (sometimes shortened to "fag") A slang term often used for gay men in particular, but also for anyone on the spectrum. Its origins are uncertain but most likely it comes from a 16th-century British use of the word to refer (sometimes disparagingly) to an old woman, particularly an older widow or single woman. Some have suggested it came from the use of the word "faggot" for bundle of sticks, referring to the kindling used to burn to people at the stake. However, this is unsubstantiated. In recent years many gay men have taken on the term with a sense of pride and will refer to themselves as fags or faggots.

Gay A term generally used to refer to homosexual men (although in some circles it can be used to refer to homosexual women or lesbians as well). It has been used for several hundred years to denote one's sexuality; in 17th-century English it was used to describe anyone who was "carefree" with their sexuality.

Gender A loaded term in that its usage varies greatly. Basically, it refers to male or female. However, some use it to refer to things such as being transgender *(see below)*, gender neutral, non-binary *(see below)*, agender (genderless), pangender (multiple genders), genderqueer (often used to mean homosexual), two-spirit *(see below)* and various other specific terms.

Heterosexual A person who is sexually attracted to persons of the opposite gender.

Homo A shortened form of the word "homosexual" often used negatively to refer to someone of the LGBTQ+ community.

Homosexual A person who is sexually attracted to persons of the same gender.

Intersex Someone who is born with certain physical characteristics of both genders, such as both a penis and vagina, or a combination of ovaries and penis, etc.

Lesbian A homosexual woman. The term comes from the Greek island of Lesbos, home to the ancient poet Sappho, who frequently wrote about her love for women and girls.

Non-Binary As the opposite of binary, this term has come to mean recognizing that there is a much wider spectrum of sexuality and gender identity than simply male and female. It is often used as an inclusive category for those who are transgender or exploring their gender expression.

Pansexual Attraction to anyone regardless of where they might fit, or see themselves, on the spectrum of gender identity or sexuality. Some see this as being the same as bisexual while others see a difference.

Queer Gay or lesbian, generally, although also occasionally used in a broader sense to include others on the spectrum. While initially used as a slang or pejorative term, it has come to be claimed quite broadly by the community and is often used as a badge of pride.

Questioning Term used to refer to those who are uncertain of their sexuality, gender, or gender expression.

Transexual This was the technical term for someone who has a form of gender identity or expression that differs from the sex they were assigned at birth. It is generally no longer used; many within the transgender community find it offensive.

Transgender The state of having a gender identity or expression different from the sex assigned at birth: for example, a person who identifies as a woman but was born with a penis, or a person born with a vagina who identifies as a man. Many – but not all – transgender persons seek a variety of surgical ways to change their sexuality to more closely resemble their gender.

Transvestite Some have seen this as the same as transgender, however, it differs substantially. It refers to someone who intentionally chooses to wear clothing that culturally is associated with the opposite gender (a man who wears a dress, a woman who wears a business suit). Obviously, the clothes worn vary considerably based on location and cultural norms. While many transvestites are also gay there are many who are heterosexual.

Two-Spirit A term that, in some Indigenous cultures of North America, is used to denote gays and lesbians. However, the term has a variety of meanings in different cultures, and in some can include anyone on the spectrum. Beyond that, there are also some Indigenous communities and language groupings that specifically reject the term claiming it is a non-Indigenous invention that has been imposed on Indigenous cultures. Others claim it has meanings in one culture, and not in others. In short, it should be used carefully and is best heard and accepted rather than simply used, especially by non-Indigenous persons.

ALSO AVAILABLE FROM WOOD LAKE

ALPHABET OF FAITH
26 Words about Faith, Ethics, and Sprituality

SARA JEWELL

Weaving together faith and culture, this breathtaking book explores what it means to live a life of faith and spirit in the 21st century. It brings together 26 "words" that reflect the challenges and joys of living in our beautiful but broken and often brutal world.

It is unwaveringly contemporary, progressive, and thought-provoking. The pieces are written for those who say they are spiritual but not religious, for people who are or may be familiar with church but perhaps don't attend anymore, for those who know Jesus and his teachings and are familiar with the Bible, even if they haven't opened it in a while.

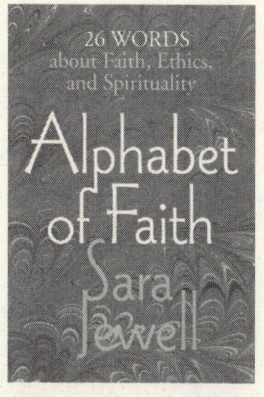

ISBN 978-1-77343-517-6
4.75" x 7" | 256 pp | Paperback | $24.95

ALSO AVAILABLE FROM WOOD LAKE

CPR FOR THE SOUL
Reviving a Sense of the Sacred in Everyday Life

TOM STELLA

"The fact that you are not dead is not sufficient proof that you are alive!" So begins Tom Stella's insightful, important, and inspiring exploration into the life, death, and rebirth of the soul. He shares the deep, eternal wisdom that knows that the lines separating the sacred and the secular, time and eternity, humanity and divinity, are false. Or, at the very least, blurred. God, by whatever name, is found in the midst of everyday life, work, and relationships. All people, all creation, and all of life is holy ground. This remarkable book offers a revival for the soul, a reminder that "we are one with something vast" – a "something" that "is not a thing or a person, but a spiritual source and force at the heart of life."

ISBN 978-1-77343-039-3
5" x 8.5" | 248 pp | Paperback | $19.95

ALSO AVAILABLE FROM WOOD LAKE

PASSION & PEACE
The Poetry of Uplift for All Occasions

COMPILED BY DIANE TUCKER

All cultures we know of, at all times, have had poetry of one sort or another — chants, songs, lullabies, epics, blessings, farewells — to mark life's most important moments, transitions, and transformations. Ever since our species began using words, we have arranged them to please, to experience the pleasures, the fun, of rhythm and rhyme, repetition and pattern. *Passion & Peace: The Poetry of Uplift for All Occasions* was compiled to speak directly to this deep human need, with 120 poems from almost as many classical and contemporary poets, and including a thematic index. A welcome addition to any library and the perfect gift for any occasion, *Passion & Peace* is a heartwarming, uplifting, and inspirational volume.

ISBN 978-1-77343-028-7
6" x 9" | 304 pp | Paperback | $24.95

WOODLAKE

Imagining, living, and telling
the faith story.

Wood Lake is the faith story company.

It has told
- the story of the seasons of the earth, the people of God, and the place and purpose of faith in the world;
- the story of the faith journey, from birth to death;
- the story of Jesus and the churches that carry his message.

Wood Lake has been telling stories for 40 years. During that time, it has given form and substance to the words, songs, pictures, and ideas of hundreds of storytellers.

Those stories have taken a multitude of forms – parables, poems, drawings, prayers, epiphanies, songs, books, paintings, hymns, curricula – all driven by a common mission of serving those on the faith journey.

WOOD LAKE PUBLISHING INC.

485 Beaver Lake Road
Kelowna, BC, Canada V4V 1S5

250.766.2778

www.woodlake.com